The Running Log and Plan Book

(size 6x9 inches.)

: Personal Information :

First Name : _______________________
last Name : _______________________
Email : _______________________
Phone : _______________________
Address : _______________________

: Emergency Contact :

First Name : _______________________
last Name : _______________________
Phone : _______________________

RUNNING / JOGGING LOG

YEAR _______ MONTH _______

DATE	DISTANCE	TIME	PACE	HR	REST HR	RUN TYPE	SHOES	NOTES

RUNNING / JOGGING LOG

YEAR _________ MONTH _________

DATE	DISTANCE	TIME	PACE	HR	REST HR	RUN TYPE	SHOES	NOTES
DATE	DISTANCE	TIME	PACE	HR	REST HR	RUN TYPE	SHOES	NOTES

SUNDAY	MONDAY	TUESDAY	WEDNESDAY	THURSDAY	FRIDAY	SATURDAY

NOTES

NOTES

RUNNING / JOGGING LOG

YEAR _______ MONTH _______

DATE	DISTANCE	TIME	PACE	HR	REST HR	RUN TYPE	SHOES	NOTES

RUNNING / JOGGING LOG

YEAR _________ MONTH _________

DATE	DISTANCE	TIME	PACE	HR	REST HR	RUN TYPE	SHOES	NOTES
DATE	DISTANCE	TIME	PACE	HR	REST HR	RUN TYPE	SHOES	NOTES

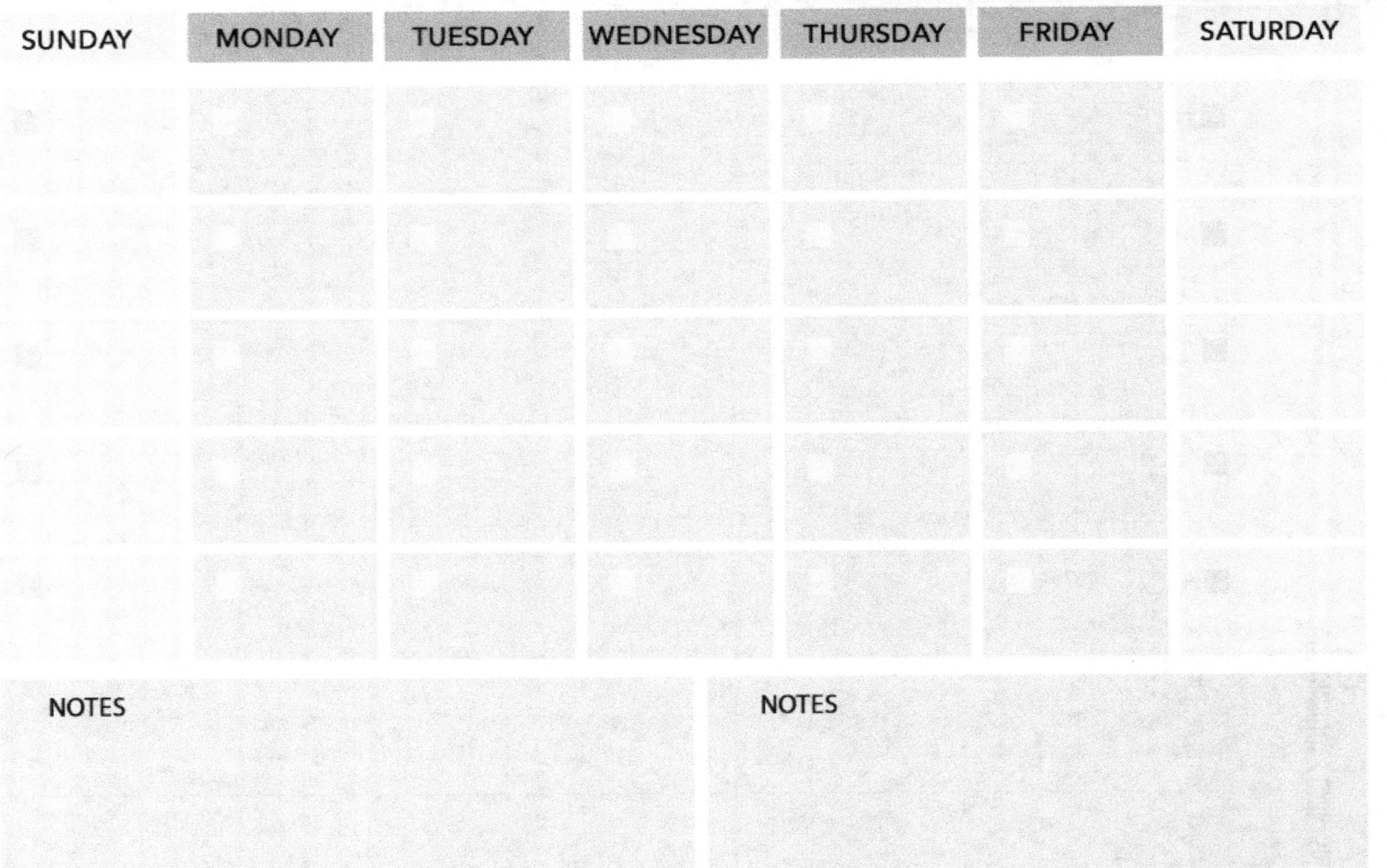
SUNDAY
MONDAY
TUESDAY
WEDNESDAY
THURSDAY
FRIDAY
SATURDAY
NOTES
NOTES

RUNNING / JOGGING LOG

YEAR _________ MONTH _________

DATE	DISTANCE	TIME	PACE	HR	REST HR	RUN TYPE	SHOES	NOTES

RUNNING / JOGGING LOG

YEAR ________ MONTH ________

DATE	DISTANCE	TIME	PACE	HR	REST HR	RUN TYPE	SHOES	NOTES

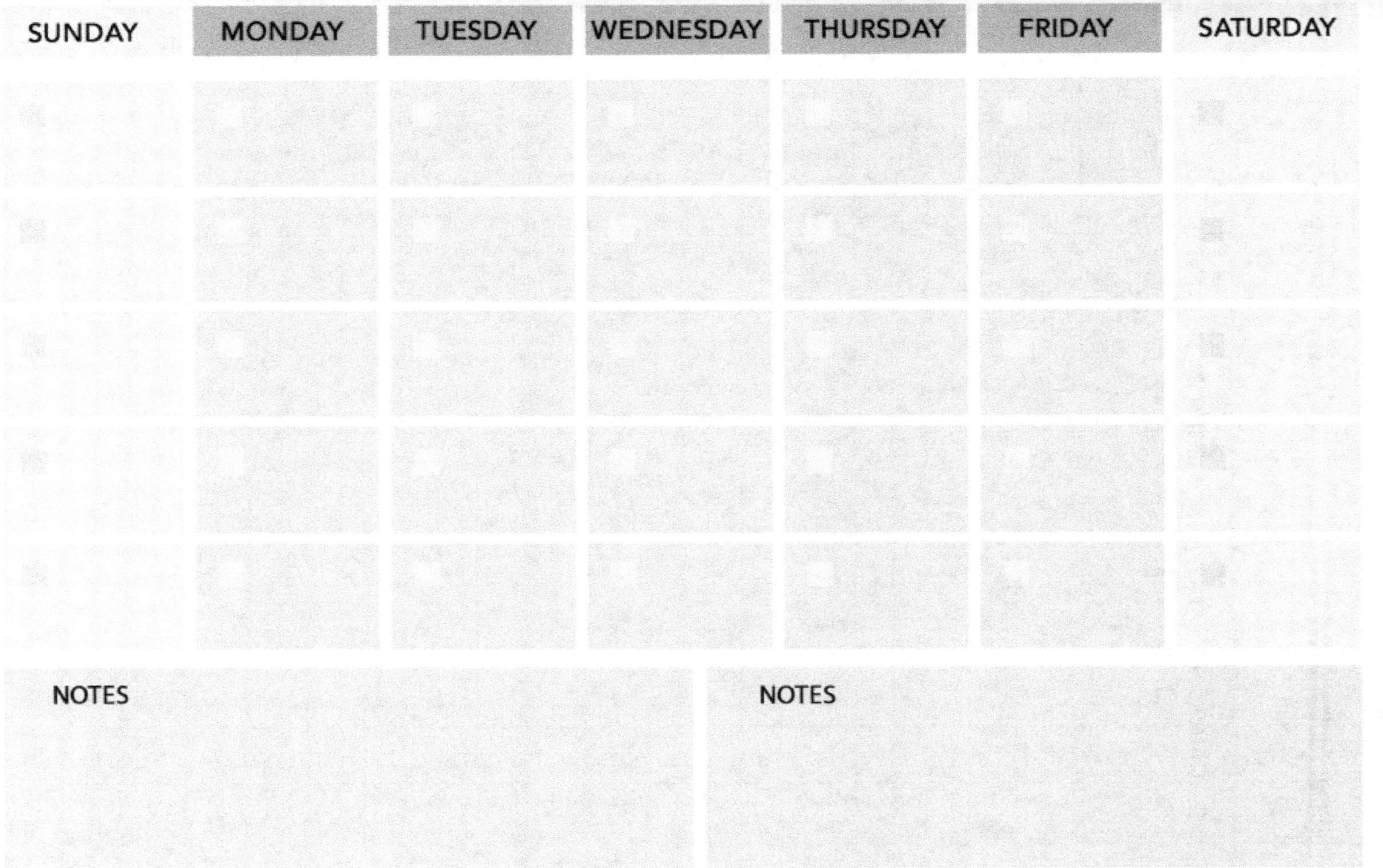

SUNDAY
MONDAY
TUESDAY
WEDNESDAY
THURSDAY
FRIDAY
SATURDAY
NOTES
NOTES

RUNNING / JOGGING LOG

YEAR _________ MONTH _________

DATE	DISTANCE	TIME	PACE	HR	REST HR	RUN TYPE	SHOES	NOTES

RUNNING / JOGGING LOG

YEAR _________ MONTH _________

DATE	DISTANCE	TIME	PACE	HR	REST HR	RUN TYPE	SHOES	NOTES
DATE	DISTANCE	TIME	PACE	HR	REST HR	RUN TYPE	SHOES	NOTES

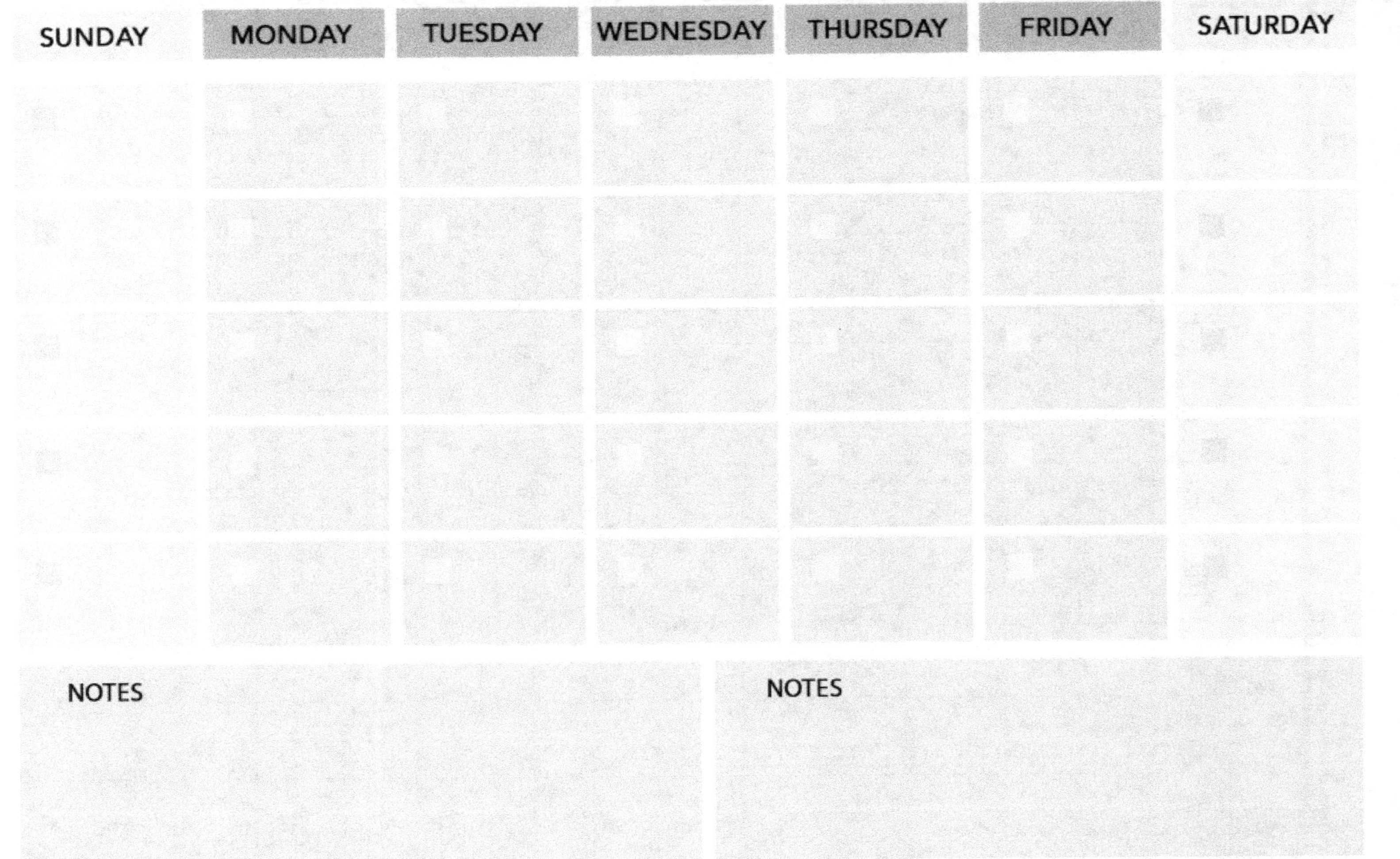
SUNDAY
MONDAY
TUESDAY
WEDNESDAY
THURSDAY
FRIDAY
SATURDAY
NOTES
NOTES

RUNNING / JOGGING LOG

YEAR _________ MONTH _________

DATE	DISTANCE	TIME	PACE	HR	REST HR	RUN TYPE	SHOES	NOTES

RUNNING / JOGGING LOG

YEAR _________ MONTH _________

DATE	DISTANCE	TIME	PACE	HR	REST HR	RUN TYPE	SHOES	NOTES
DATE	DISTANCE	TIME	PACE	HR	REST HR	RUN TYPE	SHOES	NOTES

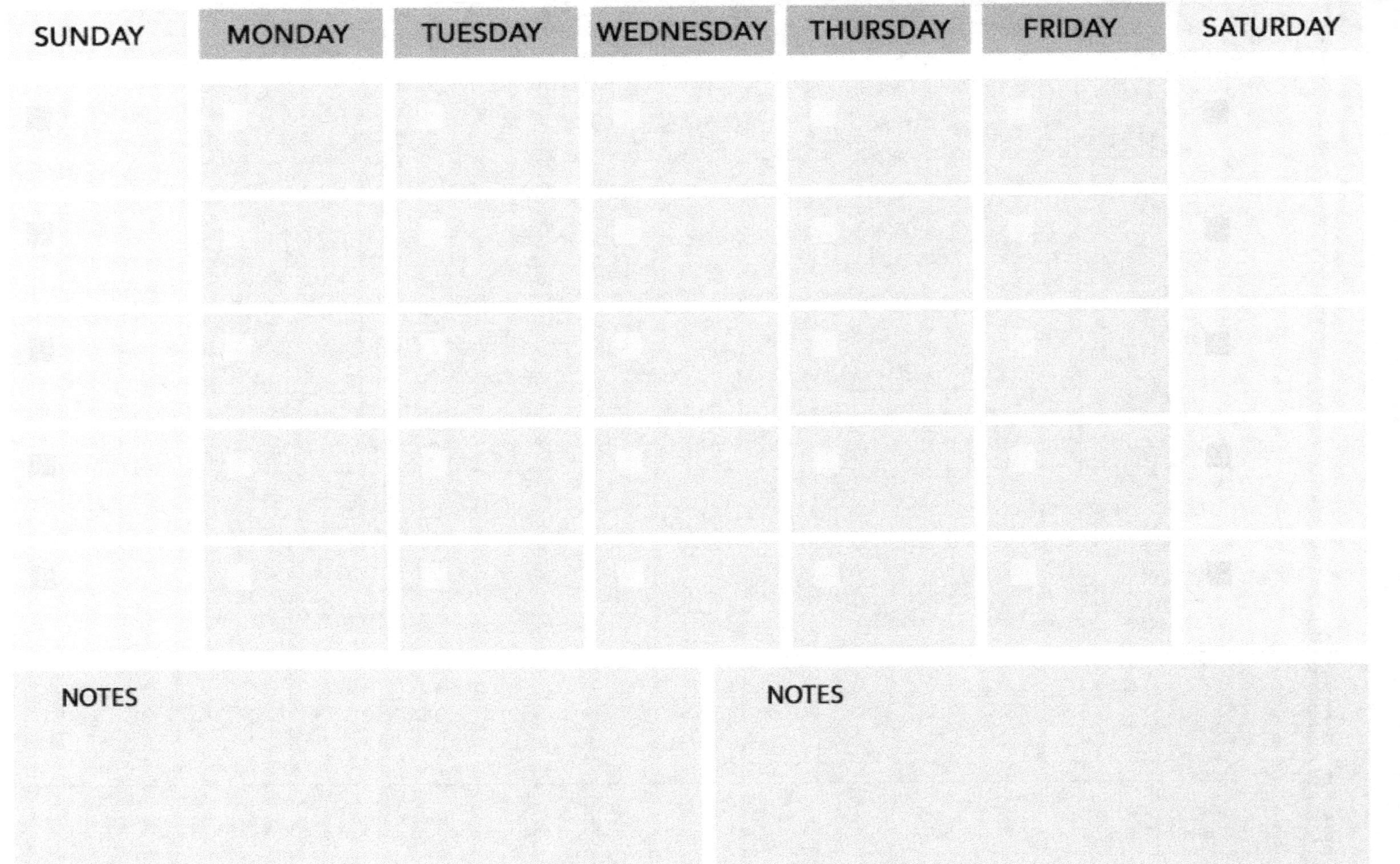

SUNDAY
MONDAY
TUESDAY
WEDNESDAY
THURSDAY
FRIDAY
SATURDAY
NOTES
NOTES

RUNNING / JOGGING LOG

YEAR _________ MONTH _________

DATE	DISTANCE	TIME	PACE	HR	REST HR	RUN TYPE	SHOES	NOTES
DATE	DISTANCE	TIME	PACE	HR	REST HR	RUN TYPE	SHOES	NOTES

RUNNING / JOGGING LOG

YEAR _________ MONTH _________

DATE	DISTANCE	TIME	PACE	HR	REST HR	RUN TYPE	SHOES	NOTES

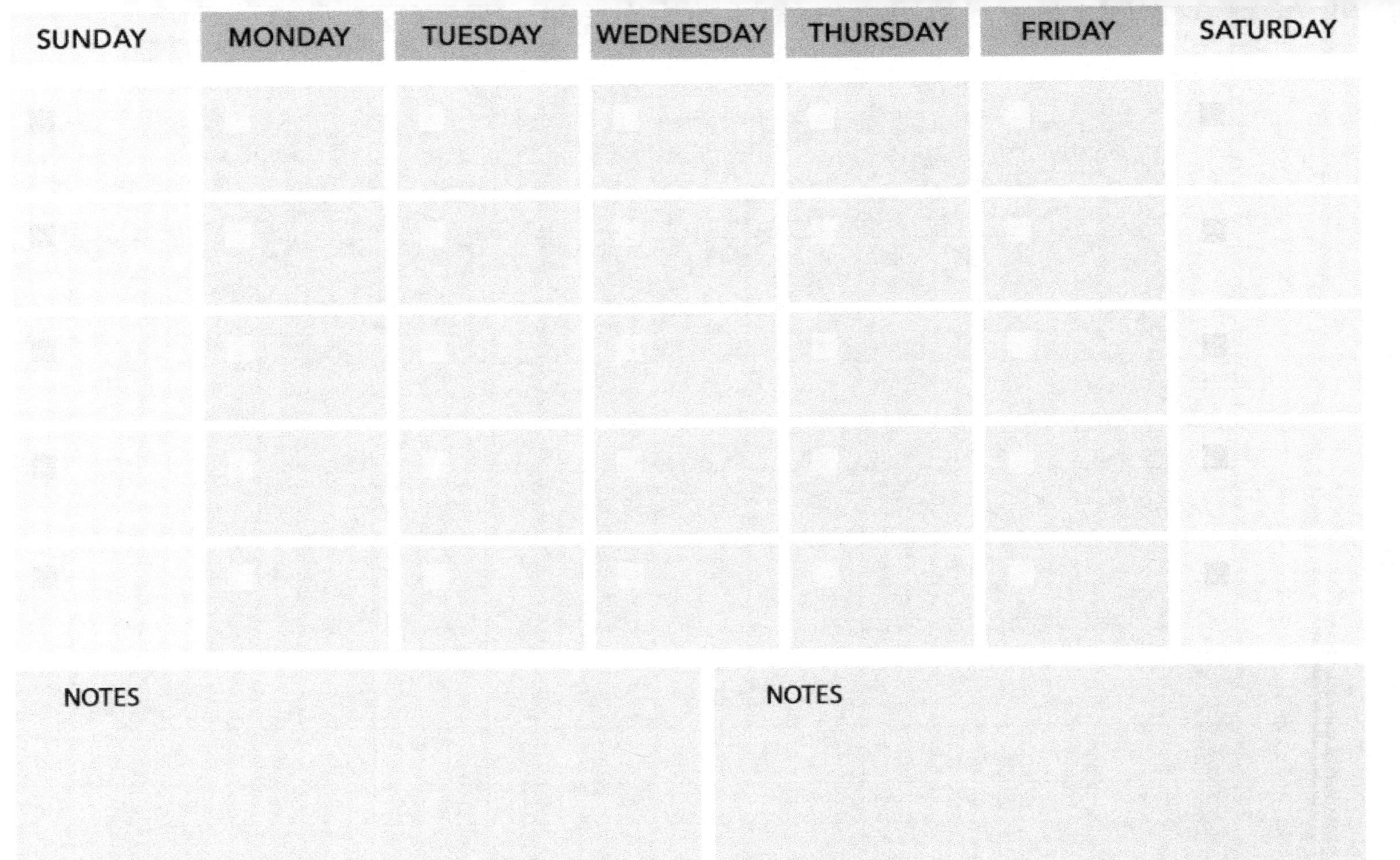

SUNDAY
MONDAY
TUESDAY
WEDNESDAY
THURSDAY
FRIDAY
SATURDAY
NOTES
NOTES

RUNNING / JOGGING LOG

YEAR _______ MONTH _______

DATE	DISTANCE	TIME	PACE	HR	REST HR	RUN TYPE	SHOES	NOTES
DATE	DISTANCE	TIME	PACE	HR	REST HR	RUN TYPE	SHOES	NOTES

RUNNING / JOGGING LOG

YEAR _________ MONTH _________

DATE	DISTANCE	TIME	PACE	HR	REST HR	RUN TYPE	SHOES	NOTES
DATE	DISTANCE	TIME	PACE	HR	REST HR	RUN TYPE	SHOES	NOTES

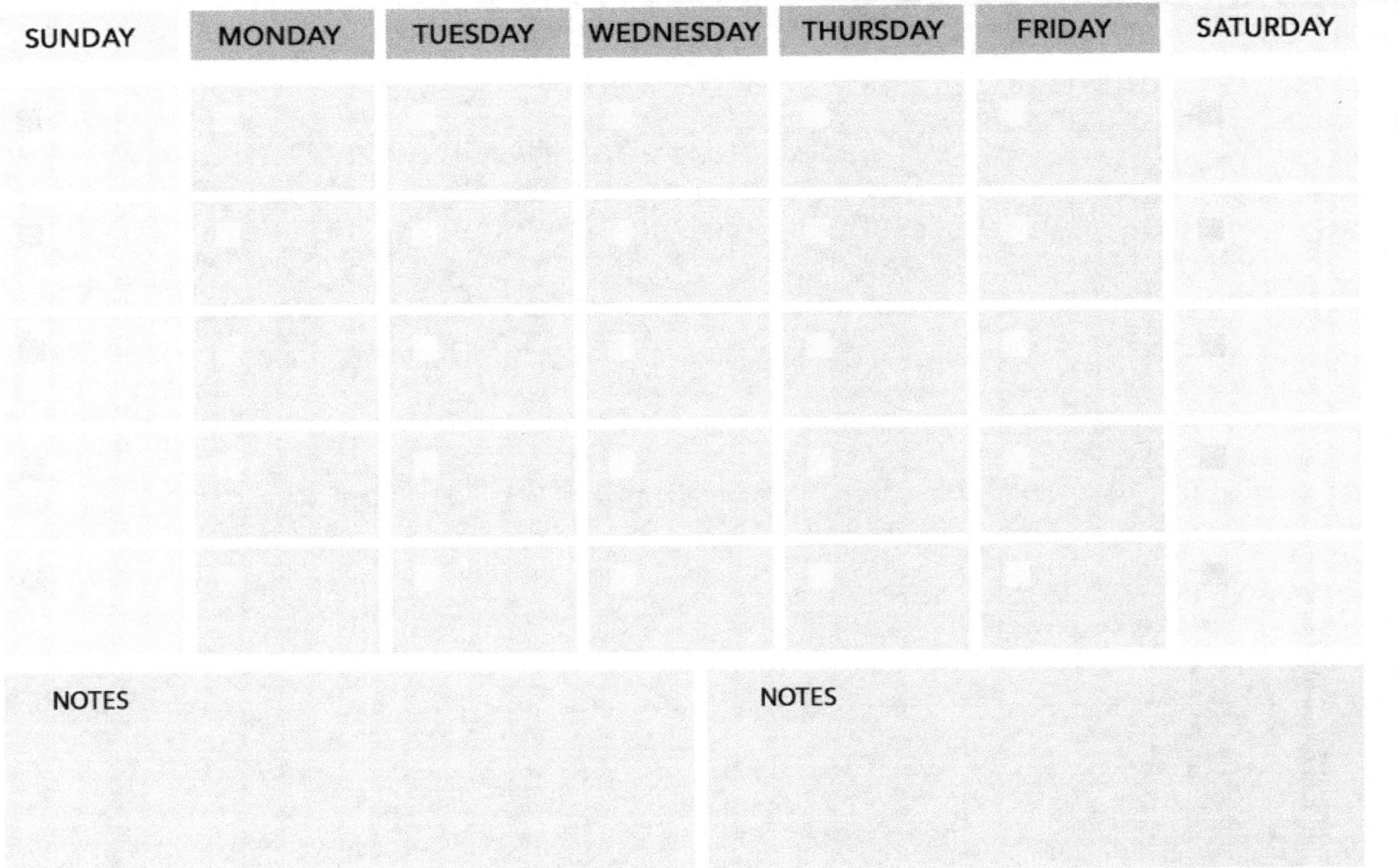

SUNDAY	MONDAY	TUESDAY	WEDNESDAY	THURSDAY	FRIDAY	SATURDAY

NOTES

NOTES

RUNNING / JOGGING LOG

YEAR ________ MONTH ________

DATE	DISTANCE	TIME	PACE	HR	REST HR	RUN TYPE	SHOES	NOTES

RUNNING / JOGGING LOG

YEAR _________ MONTH _________

DATE	DISTANCE	TIME	PACE	HR	REST HR	RUN TYPE	SHOES	NOTES

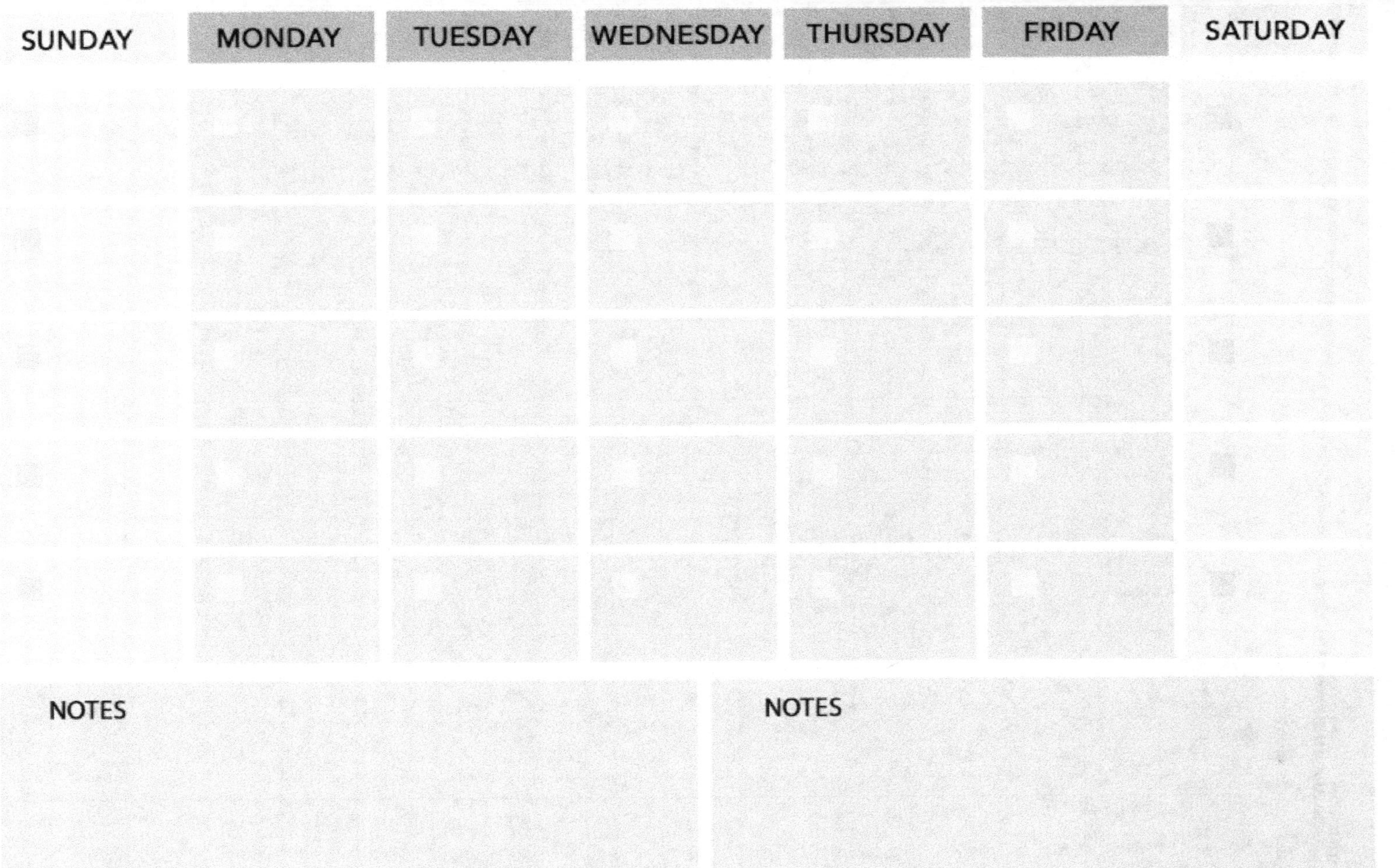

SUNDAY
MONDAY
TUESDAY
WEDNESDAY
THURSDAY
FRIDAY
SATURDAY
NOTES
NOTES

RUNNING / JOGGING LOG

YEAR _______ MONTH _______

DATE	DISTANCE	TIME	PACE	HR	REST HR	RUN TYPE	SHOES	NOTES

RUNNING / JOGGING LOG

YEAR _______ MONTH _______

DATE	DISTANCE	TIME	PACE	HR	REST HR	RUN TYPE	SHOES	NOTES

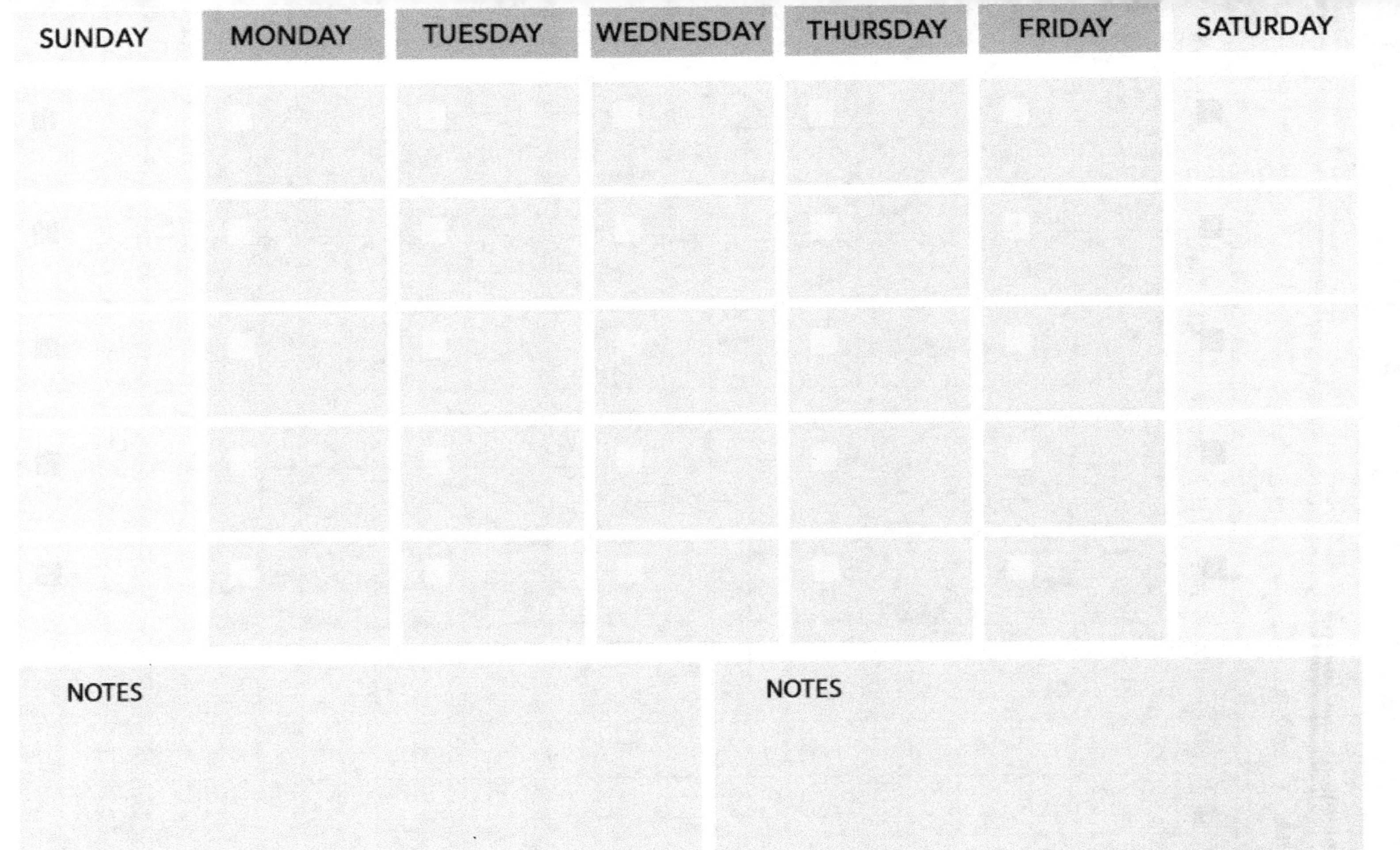

SUNDAY
MONDAY
TUESDAY
WEDNESDAY
THURSDAY
FRIDAY
SATURDAY
NOTES
NOTES

RUNNING / JOGGING LOG

YEAR _______ MONTH _______

DATE	DISTANCE	TIME	PACE	HR	REST HR	RUN TYPE	SHOES	NOTES

RUNNING / JOGGING LOG

YEAR _________ MONTH _________

DATE	DISTANCE	TIME	PACE	HR	REST HR	RUN TYPE	SHOES	NOTES
DATE	DISTANCE	TIME	PACE	HR	REST HR	RUN TYPE	SHOES	NOTES

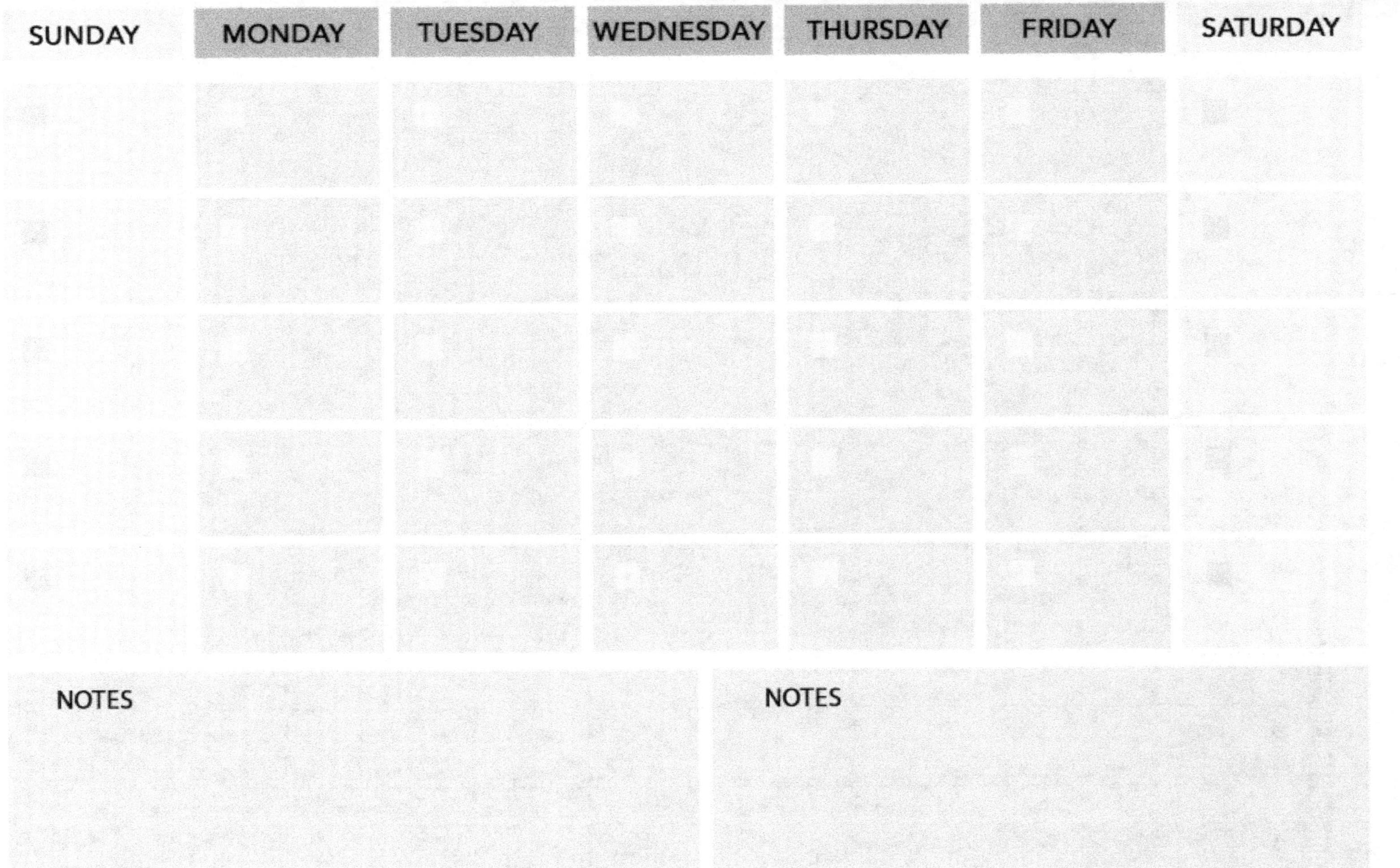

SUNDAY
MONDAY
TUESDAY
WEDNESDAY
THURSDAY
FRIDAY
SATURDAY
NOTES
NOTES

RUNNING / JOGGING LOG

YEAR _________ MONTH _________

DATE	DISTANCE	TIME	PACE	HR	REST HR	RUN TYPE	SHOES	NOTES

RUNNING / JOGGING LOG

YEAR _______ MONTH _______

DATE	DISTANCE	TIME	PACE	HR	REST HR	RUN TYPE	SHOES	NOTES
DATE	DISTANCE	TIME	PACE	HR	REST HR	RUN TYPE	SHOES	NOTES

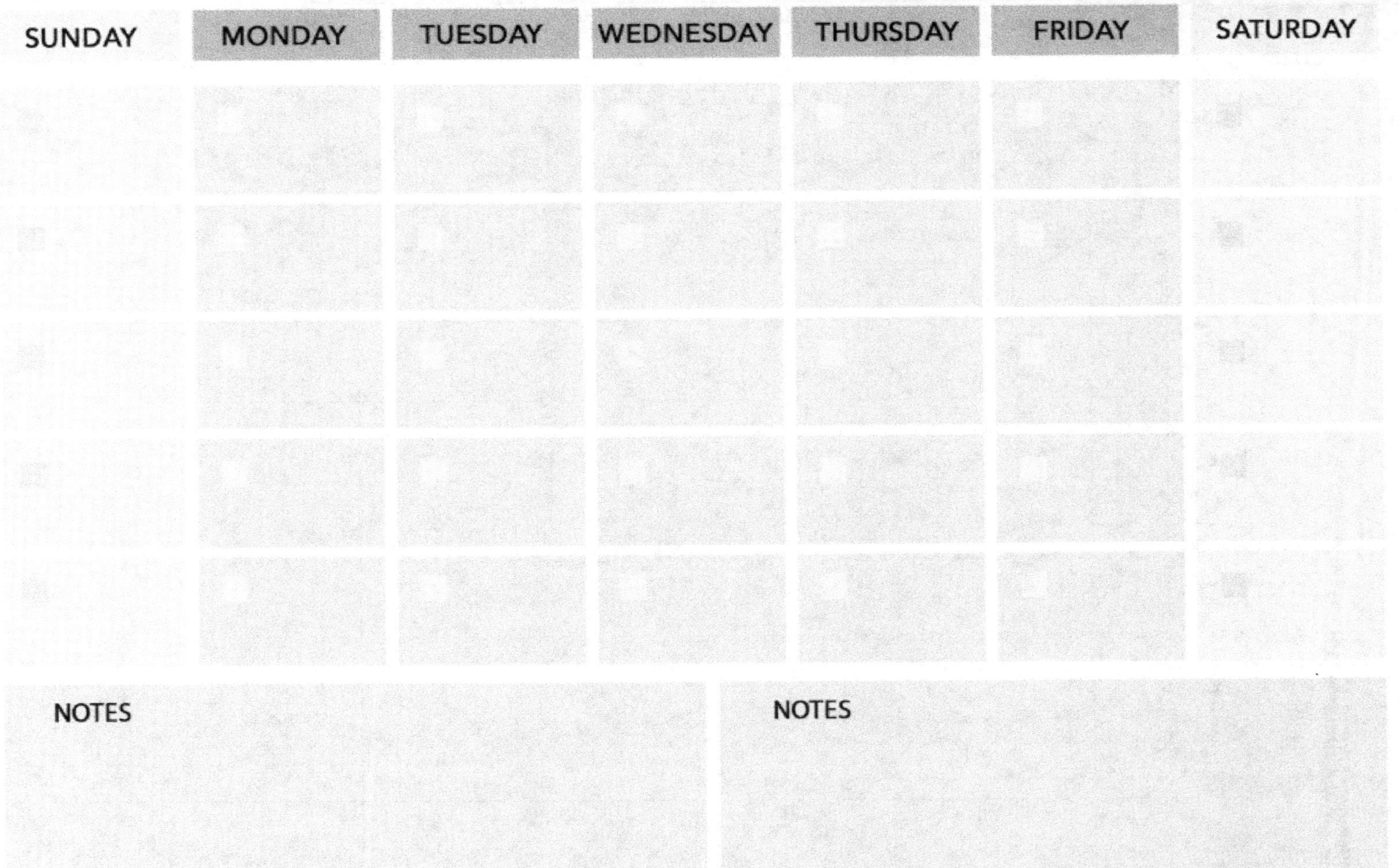

SUNDAY
MONDAY
TUESDAY
WEDNESDAY
THURSDAY
FRIDAY
SATURDAY
NOTES
NOTES

RUNNING / JOGGING LOG

YEAR __________ MONTH __________

DATE	DISTANCE	TIME	PACE	HR	REST HR	RUN TYPE	SHOES	NOTES

RUNNING / JOGGING LOG

YEAR ________ MONTH ________

DATE	DISTANCE	TIME	PACE	HR	REST HR	RUN TYPE	SHOES	NOTES

SUNDAY
MONDAY
TUESDAY
WEDNESDAY
THURSDAY
FRIDAY
SATURDAY
NOTES
NOTES

RUNNING / JOGGING LOG

YEAR _________ MONTH _________

DATE	DISTANCE	TIME	PACE	HR	REST HR	RUN TYPE	SHOES	NOTES

RUNNING / JOGGING LOG

YEAR _________ MONTH _________

DATE	DISTANCE	TIME	PACE	HR	REST HR	RUN TYPE	SHOES	NOTES
DATE	DISTANCE	TIME	PACE	HR	REST HR	RUN TYPE	SHOES	NOTES

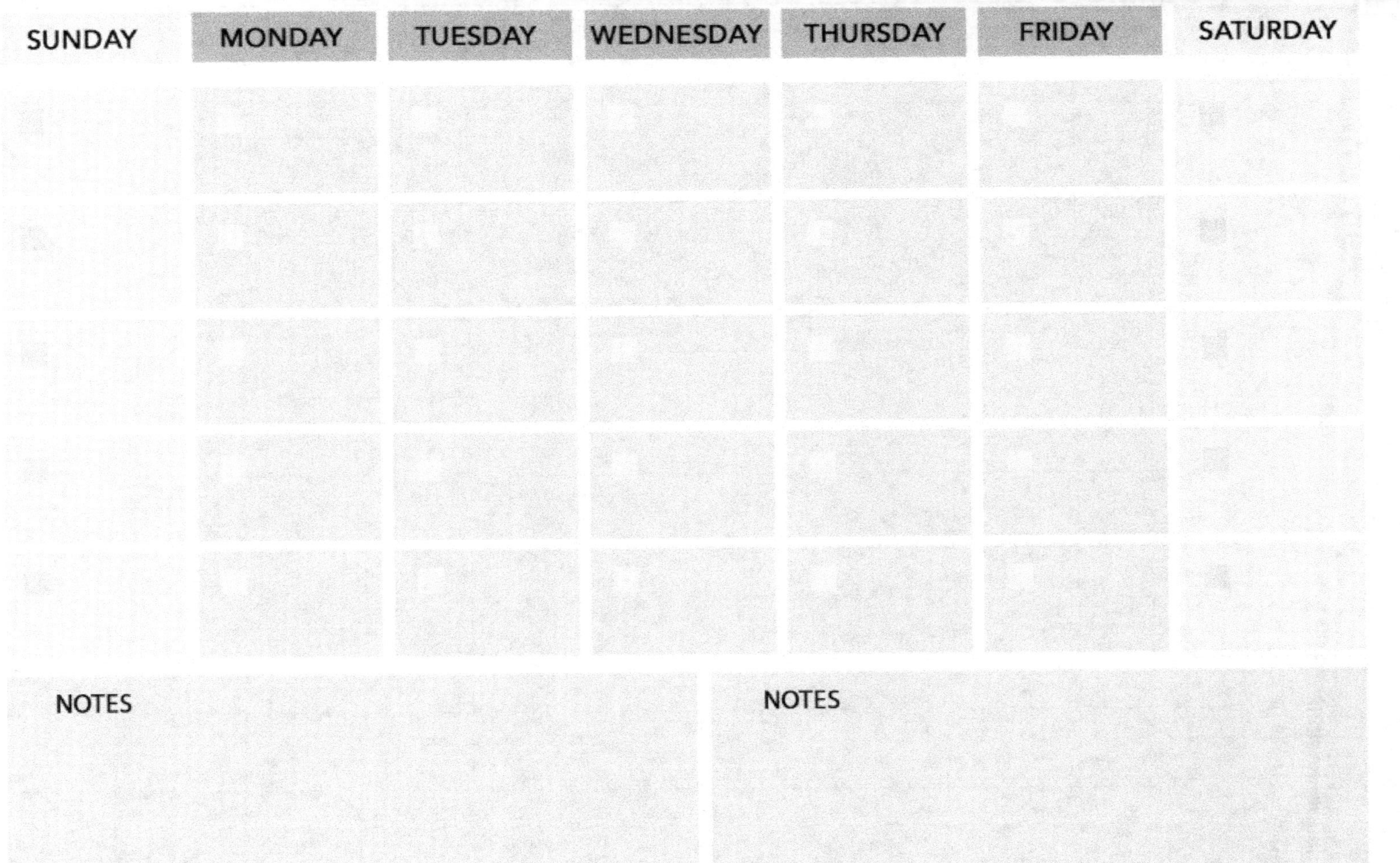

SUNDAY
MONDAY
TUESDAY
WEDNESDAY
THURSDAY
FRIDAY
SATURDAY
NOTES
NOTES

RUNNING / JOGGING LOG

YEAR _______ MONTH _______

DATE	DISTANCE	TIME	PACE	HR	REST HR	RUN TYPE	SHOES	NOTES
DATE	DISTANCE	TIME	PACE	HR	REST HR	RUN TYPE	SHOES	NOTES

RUNNING / JOGGING LOG

YEAR _________ MONTH _________

DATE	DISTANCE	TIME	PACE	HR	REST HR	RUN TYPE	SHOES	NOTES
DATE	DISTANCE	TIME	PACE	HR	REST HR	RUN TYPE	SHOES	NOTES

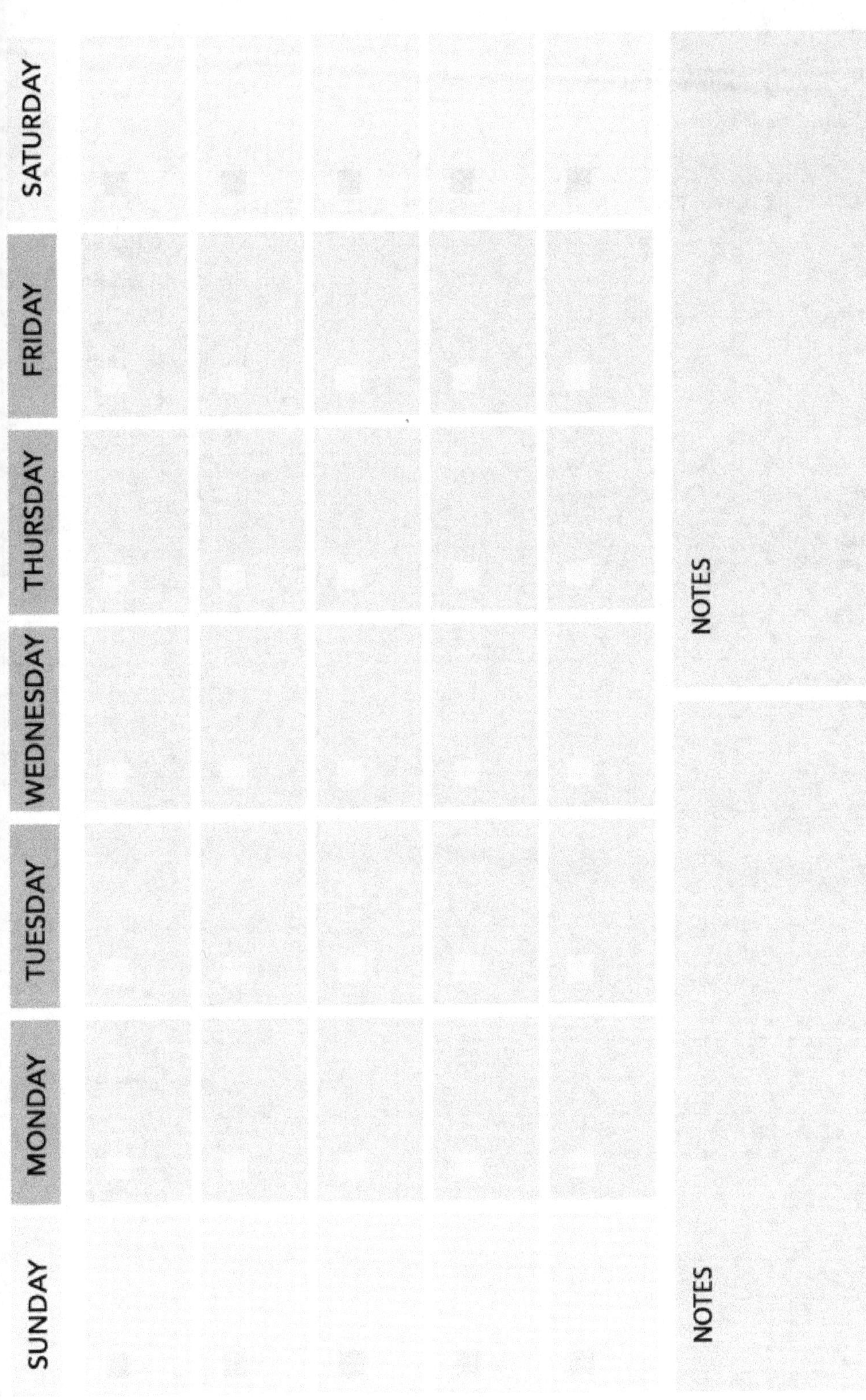

RUNNING / JOGGING LOG

YEAR _________ MONTH _________

DATE	DISTANCE	TIME	PACE	HR	REST HR	RUN TYPE	SHOES	NOTES

RUNNING / JOGGING LOG

YEAR _________ MONTH _________

DATE	DISTANCE	TIME	PACE	HR	REST HR	RUN TYPE	SHOES	NOTES
DATE	DISTANCE	TIME	PACE	HR	REST HR	RUN TYPE	SHOES	NOTES

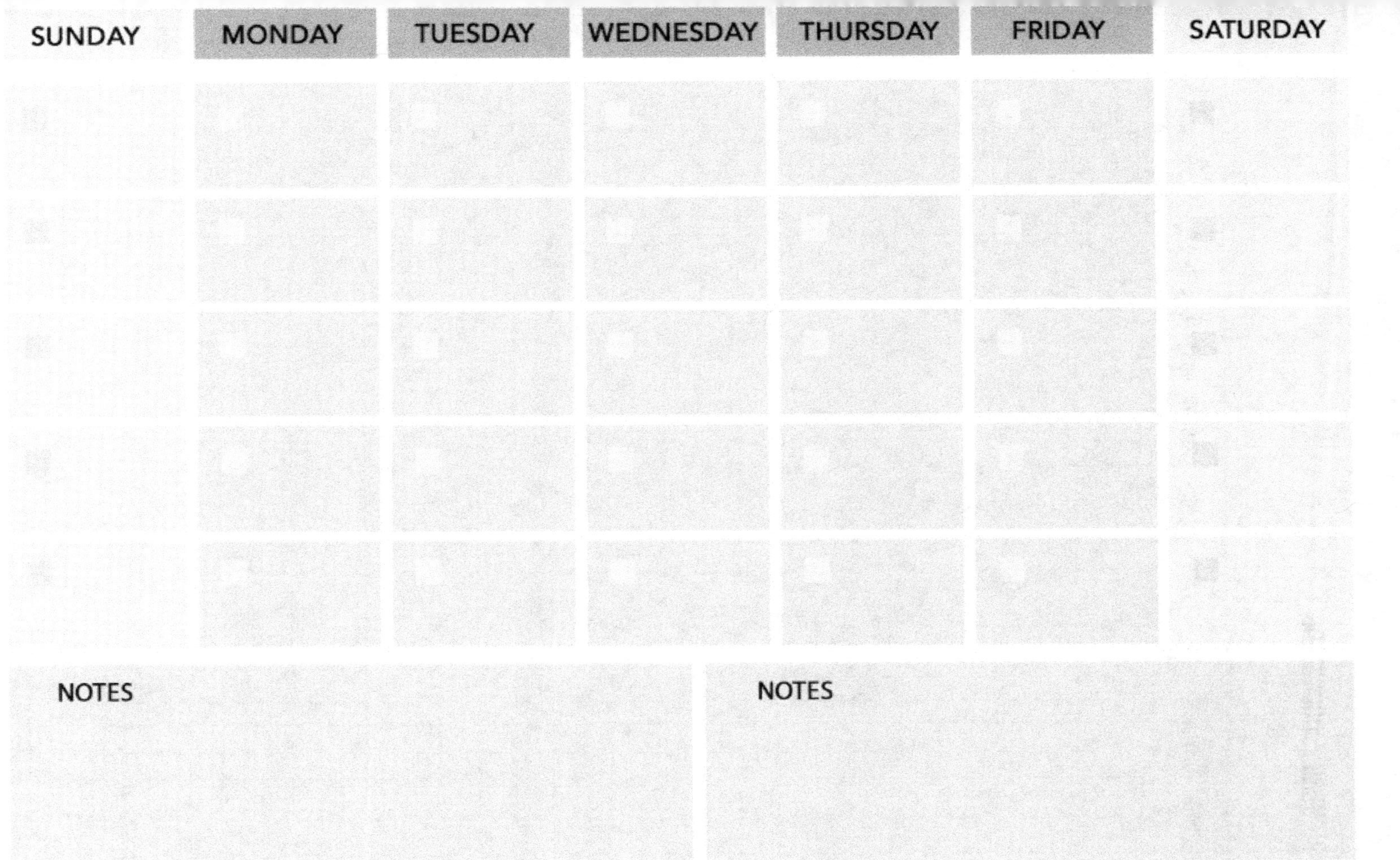
SUNDAY
MONDAY
TUESDAY
WEDNESDAY
THURSDAY
FRIDAY
SATURDAY
NOTES
NOTES

RUNNING / JOGGING LOG

YEAR _______ MONTH _______

DATE	DISTANCE	TIME	PACE	HR	REST HR	RUN TYPE	SHOES	NOTES
DATE	DISTANCE	TIME	PACE	HR	REST HR	RUN TYPE	SHOES	NOTES

RUNNING / JOGGING LOG

YEAR _________ MONTH _________

DATE	DISTANCE	TIME	PACE	HR	REST HR	RUN TYPE	SHOES	NOTES
DATE	DISTANCE	TIME	PACE	HR	REST HR	RUN TYPE	SHOES	NOTES

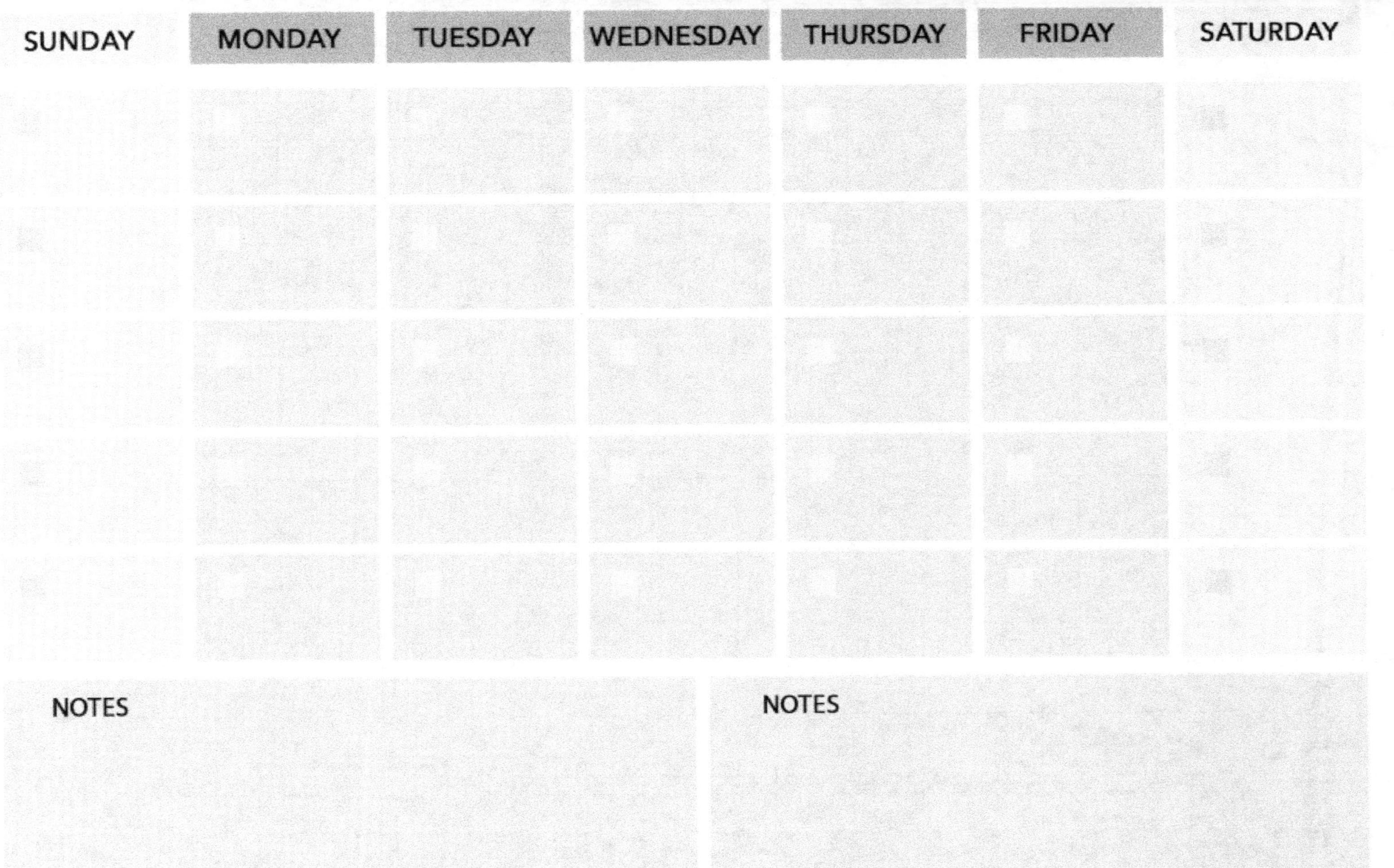

SUNDAY
MONDAY
TUESDAY
WEDNESDAY
THURSDAY
FRIDAY
SATURDAY
NOTES
NOTES

RUNNING / JOGGING LOG

YEAR ________ MONTH ________

DATE	DISTANCE	TIME	PACE	HR	REST HR	RUN TYPE	SHOES	NOTES

RUNNING / JOGGING LOG

YEAR _______ MONTH _______

DATE	DISTANCE	TIME	PACE	HR	REST HR	RUN TYPE	SHOES	NOTES
DATE	DISTANCE	TIME	PACE	HR	REST HR	RUN TYPE	SHOES	NOTES

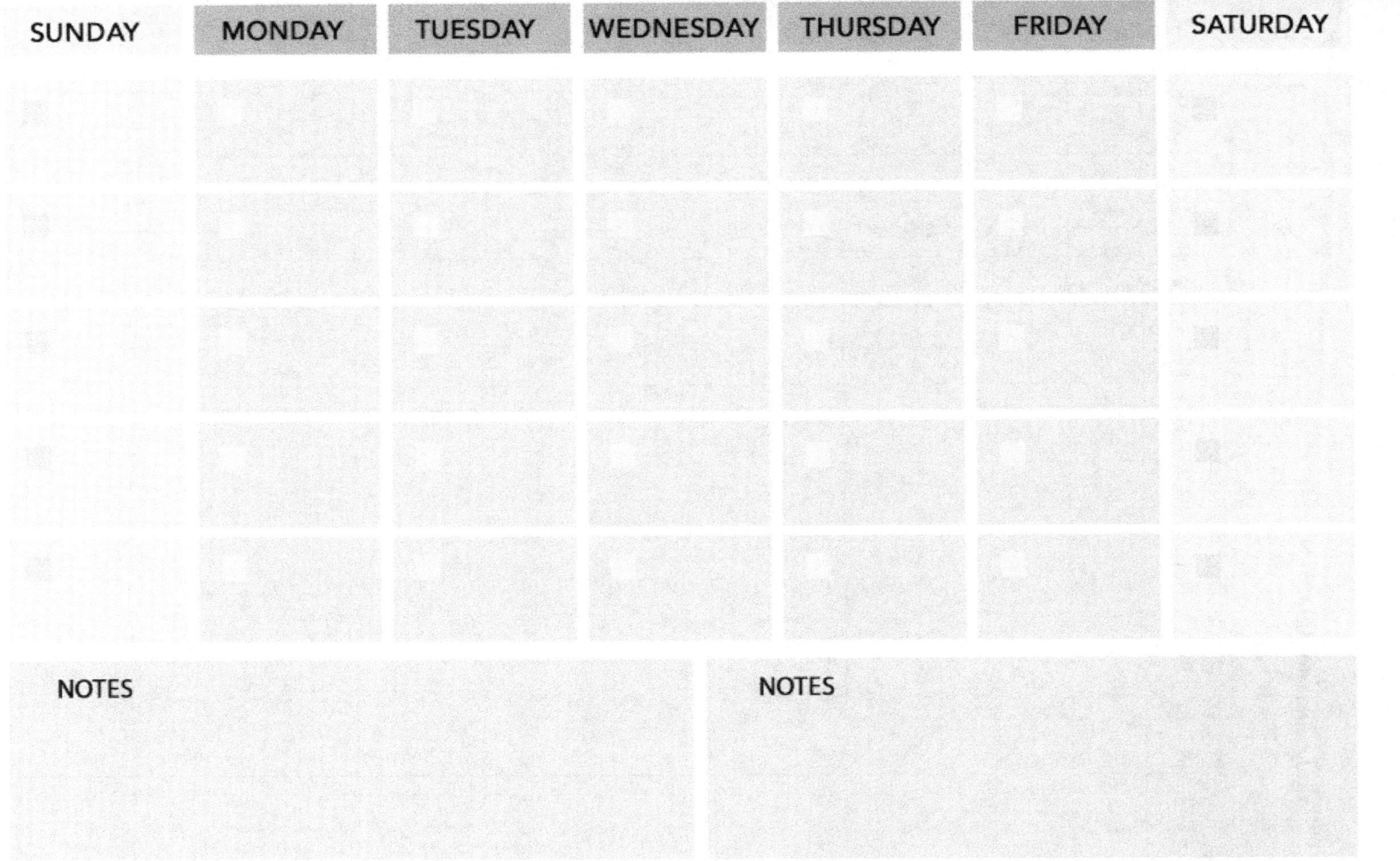

SUNDAY
MONDAY
TUESDAY
WEDNESDAY
THURSDAY
FRIDAY
SATURDAY
NOTES
NOTES

RUNNING / JOGGING LOG

YEAR _________ MONTH _________

DATE	DISTANCE	TIME	PACE	HR	REST HR	RUN TYPE	SHOES	NOTES

RUNNING / JOGGING LOG

YEAR ________ MONTH ________

DATE	DISTANCE	TIME	PACE	HR	REST HR	RUN TYPE	SHOES	NOTES

DATE	DISTANCE	TIME	PACE	HR	REST HR	RUN TYPE	SHOES	NOTES

SUNDAY
MONDAY
TUESDAY
WEDNESDAY
THURSDAY
FRIDAY
SATURDAY
NOTES
NOTES

RUNNING / JOGGING LOG

YEAR _________ MONTH _________

DATE	DISTANCE	TIME	PACE	HR	REST HR	RUN TYPE	SHOES	NOTES

RUNNING / JOGGING LOG

YEAR _________ MONTH _________

DATE	DISTANCE	TIME	PACE	HR	REST HR	RUN TYPE	SHOES	NOTES
DATE	DISTANCE	TIME	PACE	HR	REST HR	RUN TYPE	SHOES	NOTES

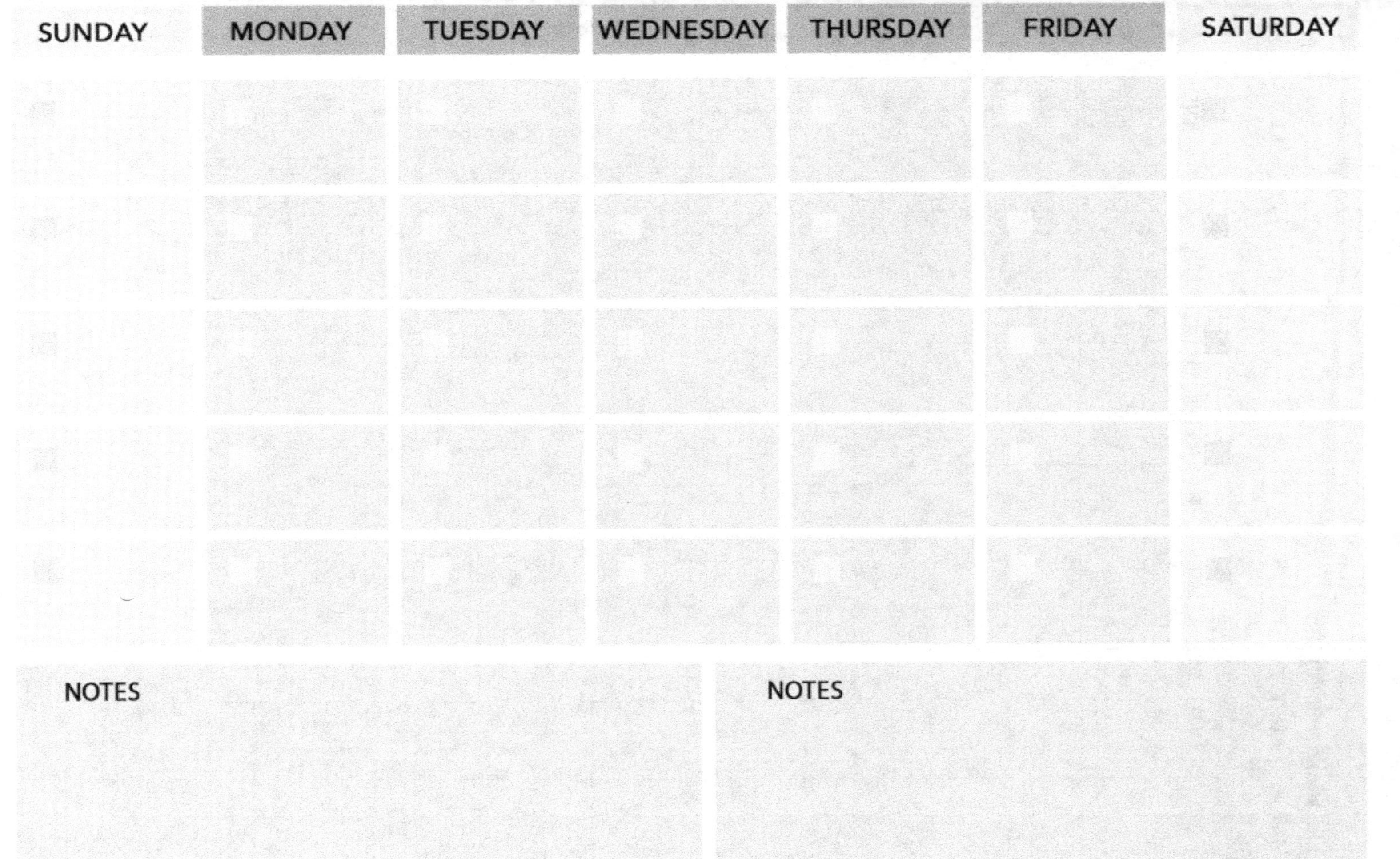

SUNDAY
MONDAY
TUESDAY
WEDNESDAY
THURSDAY
FRIDAY
SATURDAY
NOTES
NOTES

RUNNING / JOGGING LOG

YEAR _______ MONTH _______

DATE	DISTANCE	TIME	PACE	HR	REST HR	RUN TYPE	SHOES	NOTES

RUNNING / JOGGING LOG

YEAR _________ MONTH _________

DATE	DISTANCE	TIME	PACE	HR	REST HR	RUN TYPE	SHOES	NOTES
DATE	DISTANCE	TIME	PACE	HR	REST HR	RUN TYPE	SHOES	NOTES

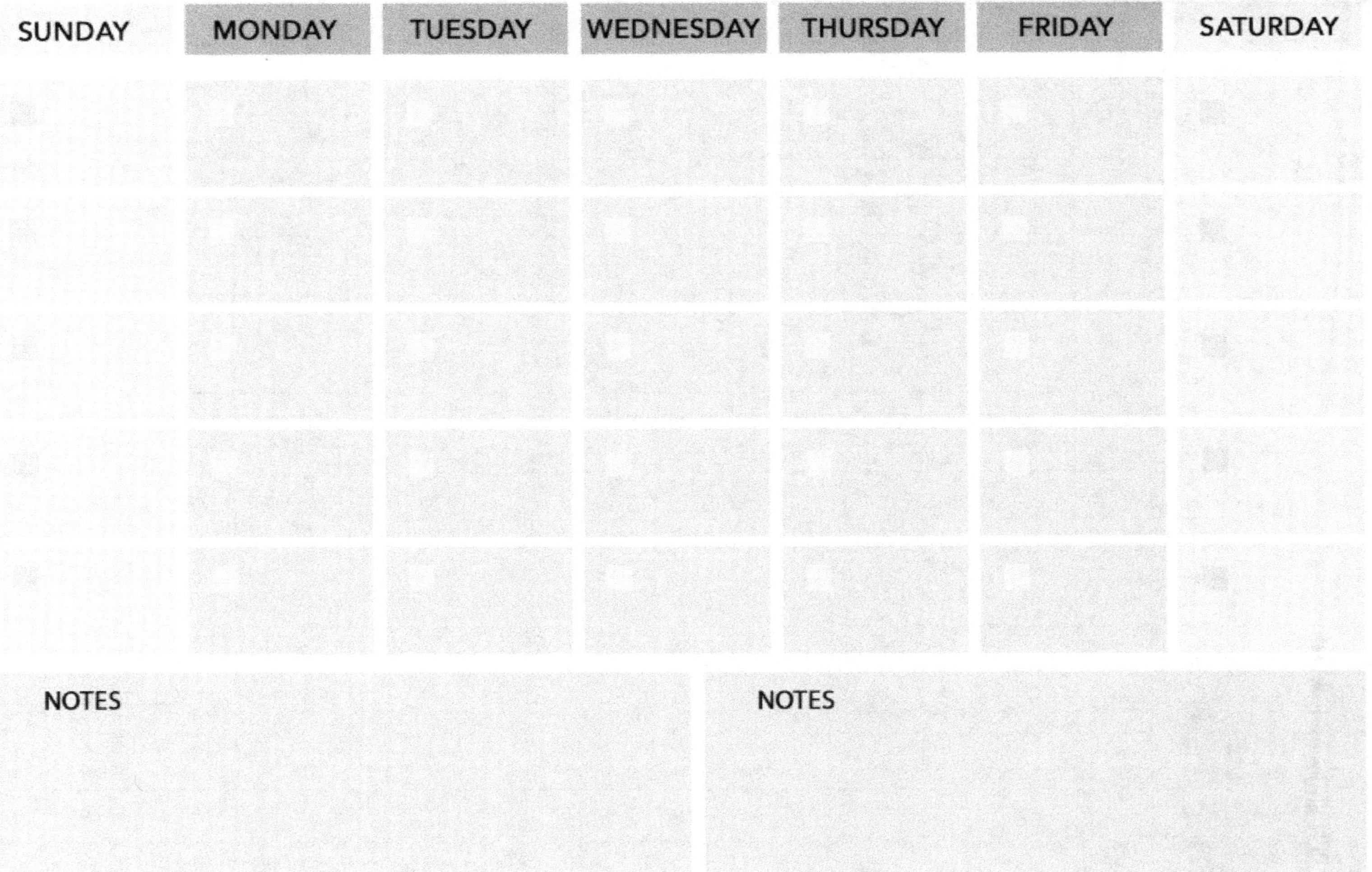

SUNDAY
MONDAY
TUESDAY
WEDNESDAY
THURSDAY
FRIDAY
SATURDAY
NOTES
NOTES

RUNNING / JOGGING LOG

YEAR _______ MONTH _______

DATE	DISTANCE	TIME	PACE	HR	REST HR	RUN TYPE	SHOES	NOTES
DATE	DISTANCE	TIME	PACE	HR	REST HR	RUN TYPE	SHOES	NOTES

RUNNING / JOGGING LOG

YEAR _________ MONTH _________

DATE	DISTANCE	TIME	PACE	HR	REST HR	RUN TYPE	SHOES	NOTES
DATE	DISTANCE	TIME	PACE	HR	REST HR	RUN TYPE	SHOES	NOTES

SUNDAY	MONDAY	TUESDAY	WEDNESDAY	THURSDAY	FRIDAY	SATURDAY

NOTES

NOTES

RUNNING / JOGGING LOG

YEAR _________ MONTH _________

DATE	DISTANCE	TIME	PACE	HR	REST HR	RUN TYPE	SHOES	NOTES

RUNNING / JOGGING LOG

YEAR _________ MONTH _________

DATE	DISTANCE	TIME	PACE	HR	REST HR	RUN TYPE	SHOES	NOTES
DATE	DISTANCE	TIME	PACE	HR	REST HR	RUN TYPE	SHOES	NOTES

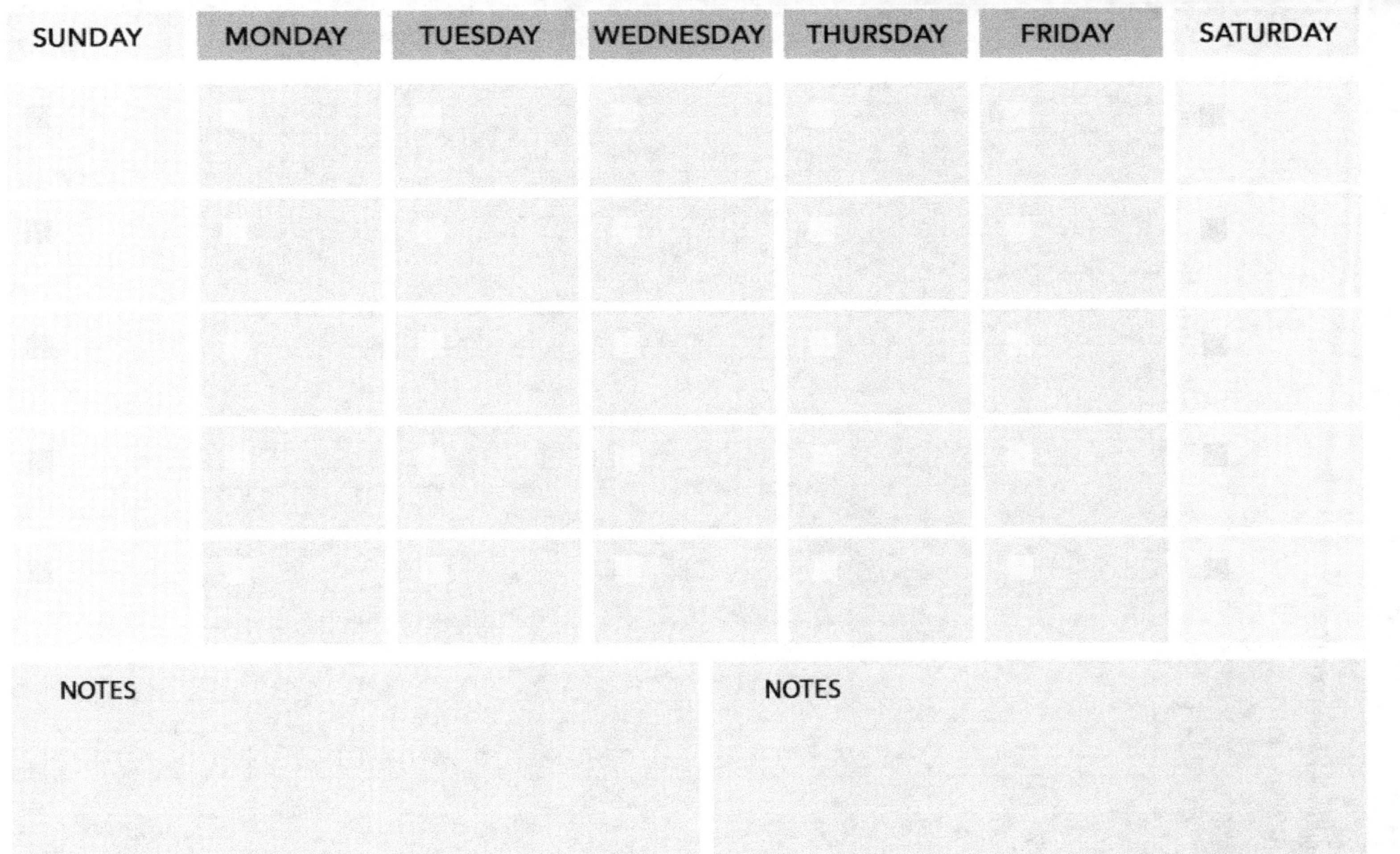

SUNDAY
MONDAY
TUESDAY
WEDNESDAY
THURSDAY
FRIDAY
SATURDAY
NOTES
NOTES

RUNNING / JOGGING LOG

YEAR _______ MONTH _______

DATE	DISTANCE	TIME	PACE	HR	REST HR	RUN TYPE	SHOES	NOTES

RUNNING / JOGGING LOG

YEAR _________ MONTH _________

DATE	DISTANCE	TIME	PACE	HR	REST HR	RUN TYPE	SHOES	NOTES

DATE	DISTANCE	TIME	PACE	HR	REST HR	RUN TYPE	SHOES	NOTES

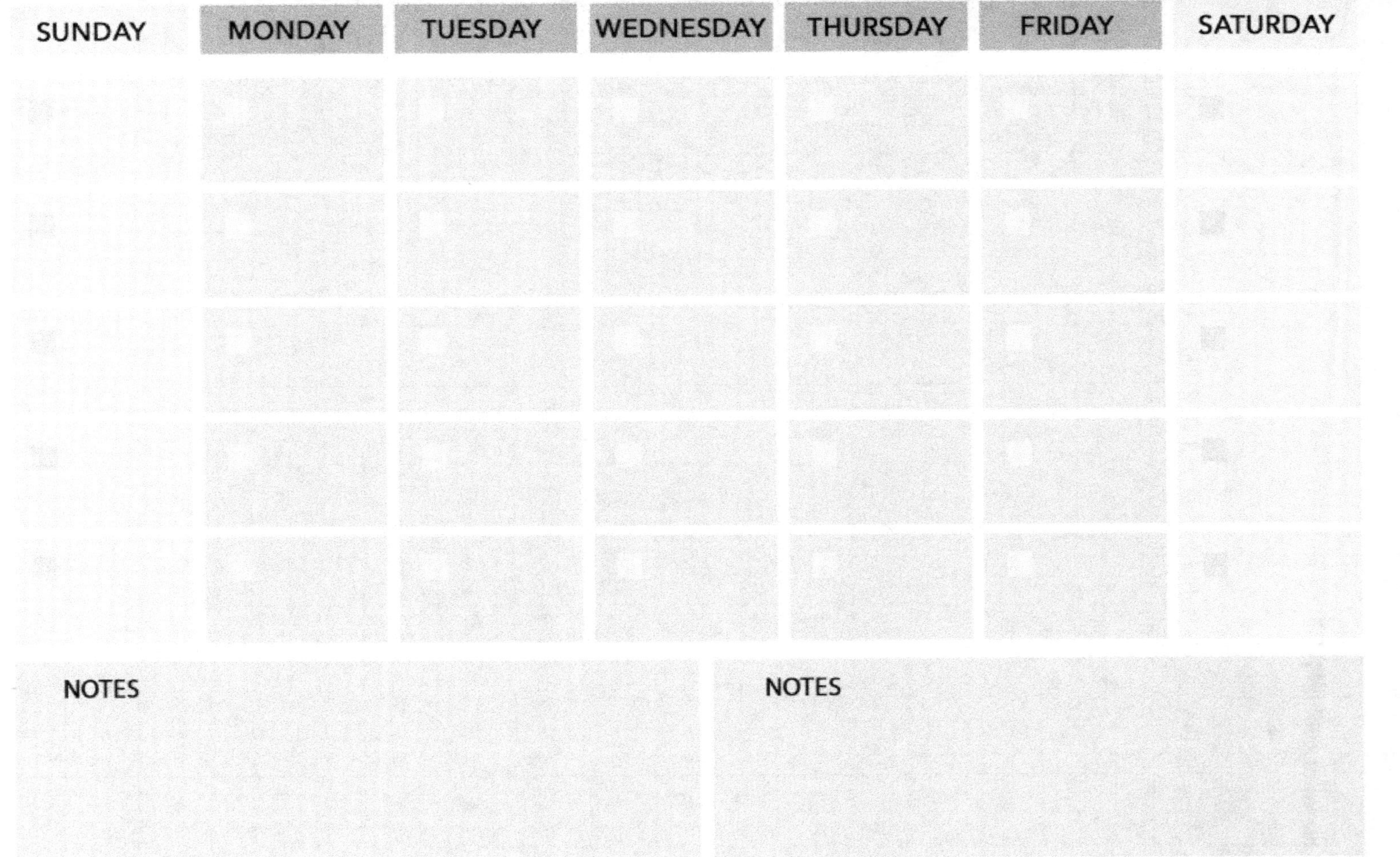

SUNDAY
MONDAY
TUESDAY
WEDNESDAY
THURSDAY
FRIDAY
SATURDAY
NOTES
NOTES

RUNNING / JOGGING LOG

YEAR _________ MONTH _________

DATE	DISTANCE	TIME	PACE	HR	REST HR	RUN TYPE	SHOES	NOTES

RUNNING / JOGGING LOG

YEAR _________ MONTH _________

DATE	DISTANCE	TIME	PACE	HR	REST HR	RUN TYPE	SHOES	NOTES
DATE	DISTANCE	TIME	PACE	HR	REST HR	RUN TYPE	SHOES	NOTES

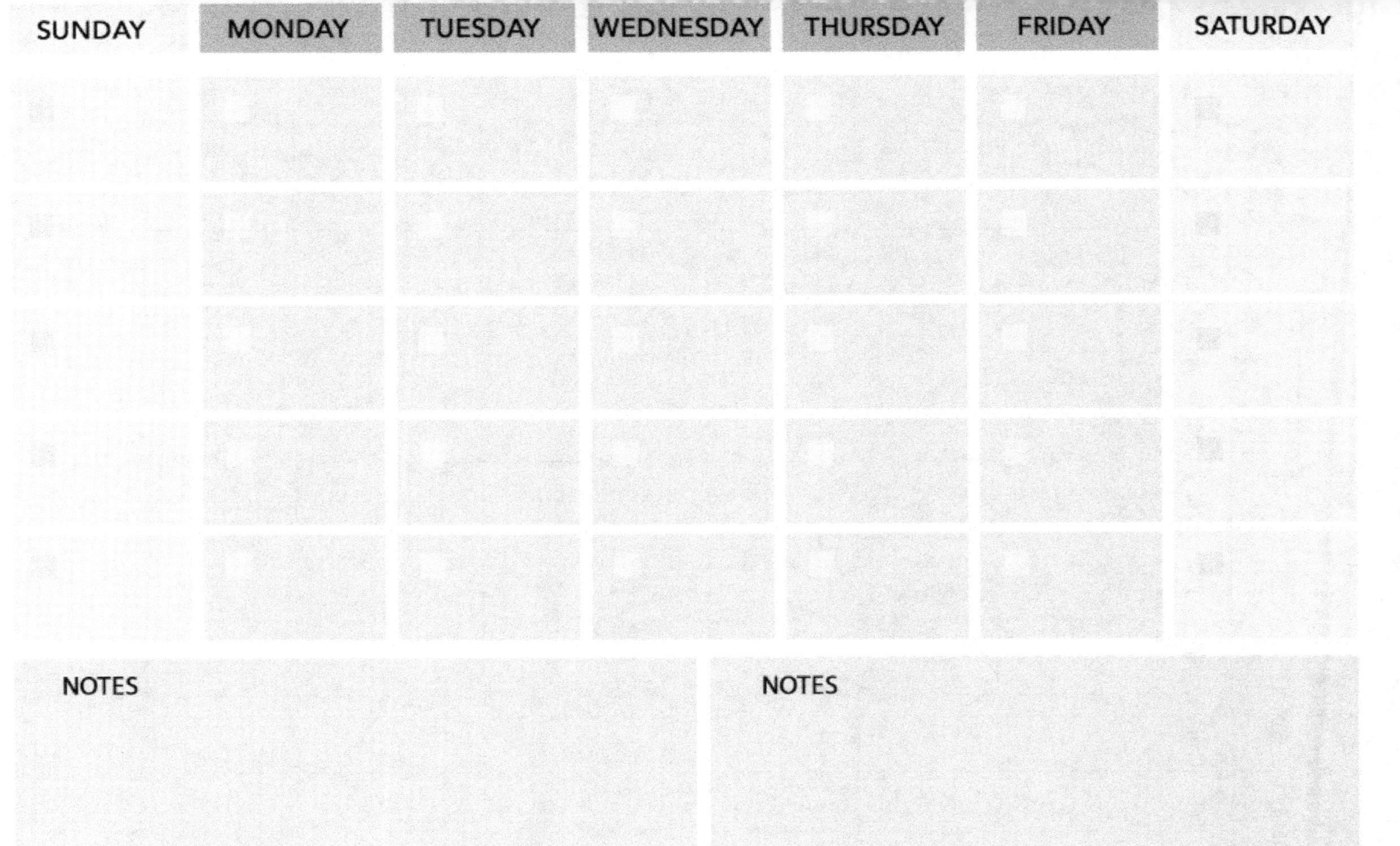

SUNDAY
MONDAY
TUESDAY
WEDNESDAY
THURSDAY
FRIDAY
SATURDAY
NOTES
NOTES

RUNNING / JOGGING LOG

YEAR _________ MONTH _________

DATE	DISTANCE	TIME	PACE	HR	REST HR	RUN TYPE	SHOES	NOTES

RUNNING / JOGGING LOG

YEAR _________ MONTH _________

DATE	DISTANCE	TIME	PACE	HR	REST HR	RUN TYPE	SHOES	NOTES
DATE	DISTANCE	TIME	PACE	HR	REST HR	RUN TYPE	SHOES	NOTES

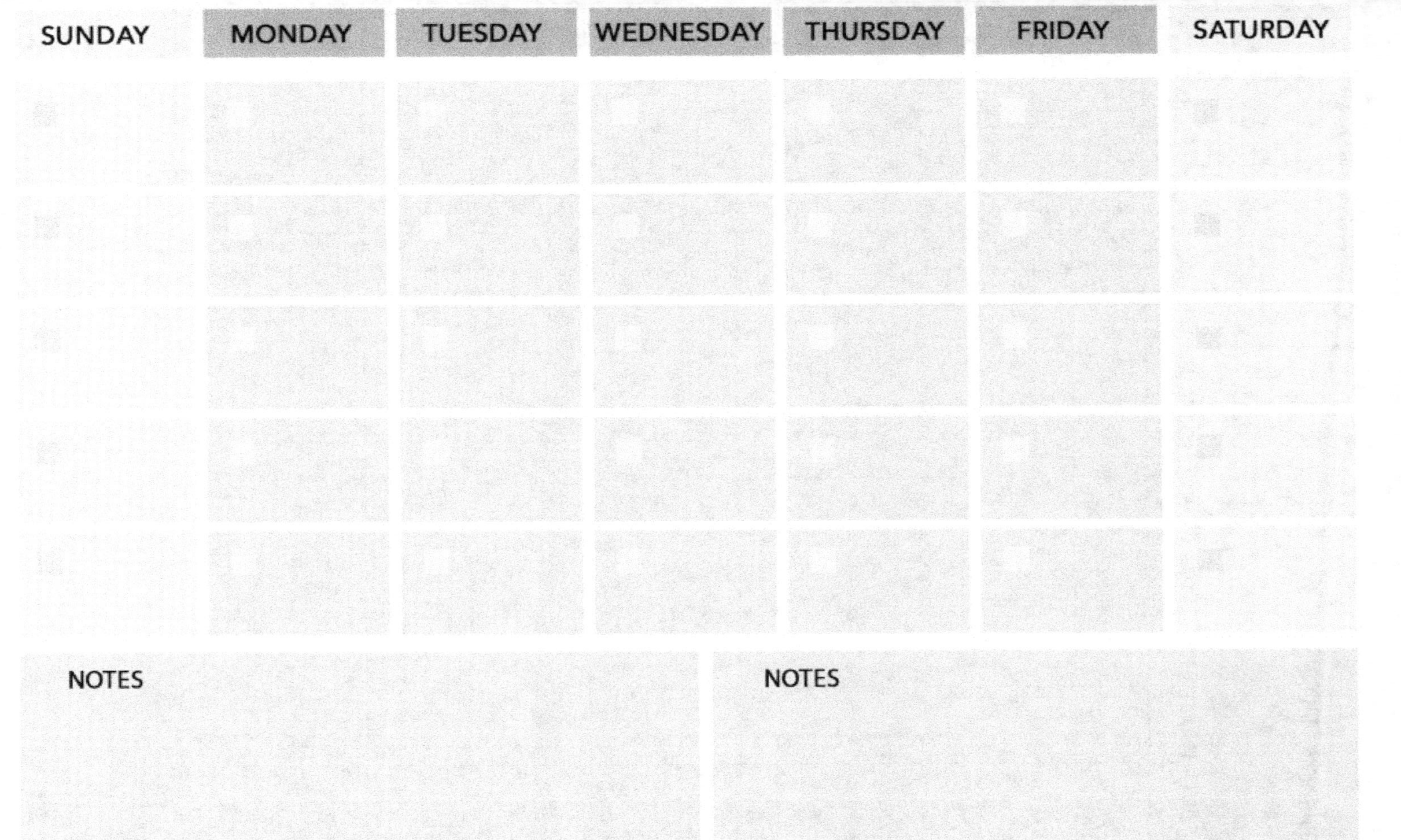

SUNDAY
MONDAY
TUESDAY
WEDNESDAY
THURSDAY
FRIDAY
SATURDAY
NOTES
NOTES

RUNNING / JOGGING LOG

YEAR _________ MONTH _________

DATE	DISTANCE	TIME	PACE	HR	REST HR	RUN TYPE	SHOES	NOTES

RUNNING / JOGGING LOG

YEAR _________ MONTH _________

DATE	DISTANCE	TIME	PACE	HR	REST HR	RUN TYPE	SHOES	NOTES
DATE	DISTANCE	TIME	PACE	HR	REST HR	RUN TYPE	SHOES	NOTES

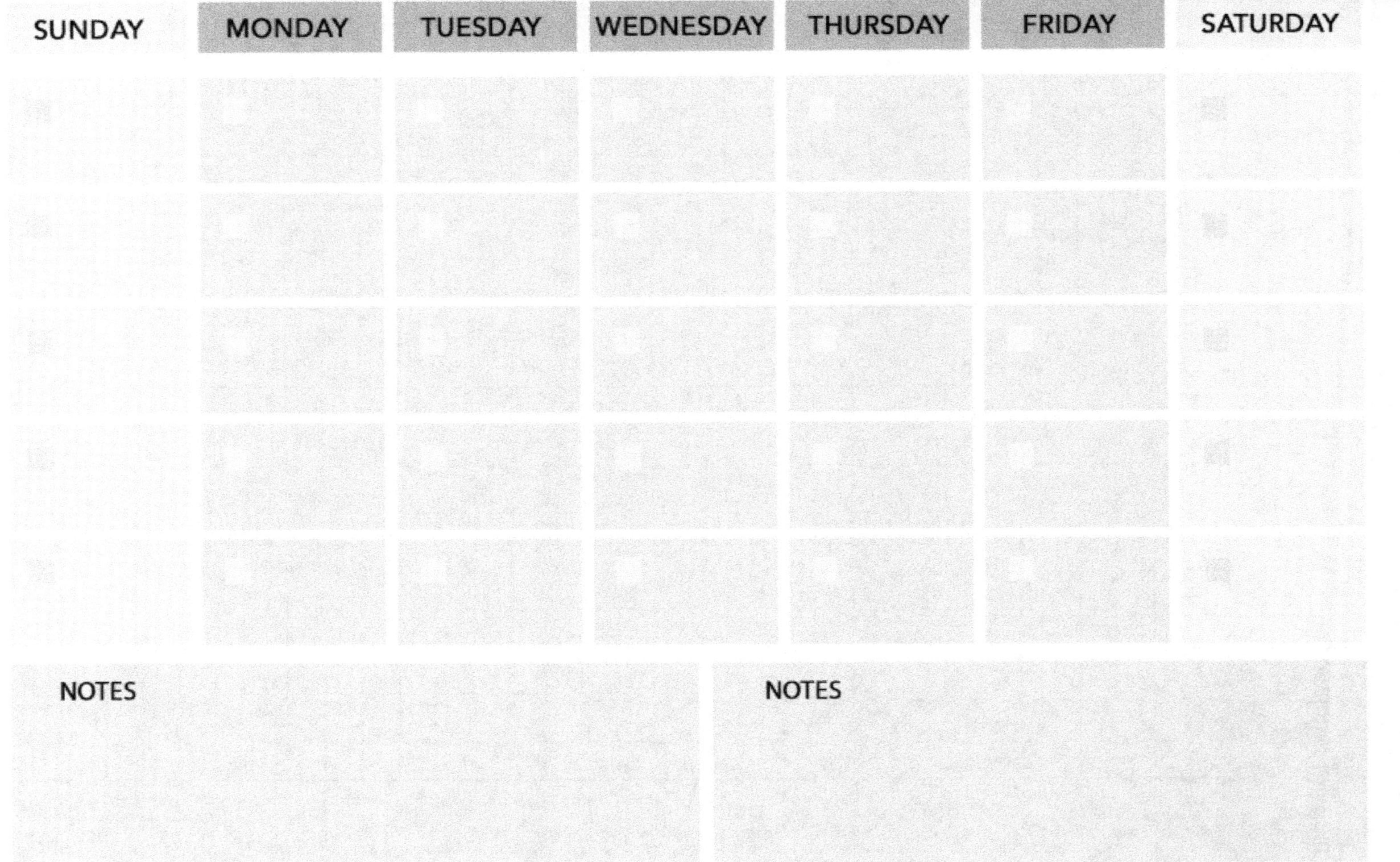

SUNDAY
MONDAY
TUESDAY
WEDNESDAY
THURSDAY
FRIDAY
SATURDAY
NOTES
NOTES

RUNNING / JOGGING LOG

YEAR _________ MONTH _________

DATE	DISTANCE	TIME	PACE	HR	REST HR	RUN TYPE	SHOES	NOTES
DATE	DISTANCE	TIME	PACE	HR	REST HR	RUN TYPE	SHOES	NOTES

RUNNING / JOGGING LOG

YEAR _______ MONTH _______

DATE	DISTANCE	TIME	PACE	HR	REST HR	RUN TYPE	SHOES	NOTES

DATE	DISTANCE	TIME	PACE	HR	REST HR	RUN TYPE	SHOES	NOTES

SUNDAY
MONDAY
TUESDAY
WEDNESDAY
THURSDAY
FRIDAY
SATURDAY
NOTES
NOTES

RUNNING / JOGGING LOG

YEAR _________ MONTH _________

DATE	DISTANCE	TIME	PACE	HR	REST HR	RUN TYPE	SHOES	NOTES

RUNNING / JOGGING LOG

YEAR _________ MONTH _________

DATE	DISTANCE	TIME	PACE	HR	REST HR	RUN TYPE	SHOES	NOTES

DATE	DISTANCE	TIME	PACE	HR	REST HR	RUN TYPE	SHOES	NOTES

SUNDAY	MONDAY	TUESDAY	WEDNESDAY	THURSDAY	FRIDAY	SATURDAY

NOTES

NOTES

RUNNING / JOGGING LOG

YEAR _________ MONTH _________

DATE	DISTANCE	TIME	PACE	HR	REST HR	RUN TYPE	SHOES	NOTES
DATE	DISTANCE	TIME	PACE	HR	REST HR	RUN TYPE	SHOES	NOTES

RUNNING / JOGGING LOG

YEAR _________ MONTH _________

DATE	DISTANCE	TIME	PACE	HR	REST HR	RUN TYPE	SHOES	NOTES

SUNDAY
MONDAY
TUESDAY
WEDNESDAY
THURSDAY
FRIDAY
SATURDAY
NOTES
NOTES

RUNNING / JOGGING LOG

YEAR _________ MONTH _________

DATE	DISTANCE	TIME	PACE	HR	REST HR	RUN TYPE	SHOES	NOTES
DATE	DISTANCE	TIME	PACE	HR	REST HR	RUN TYPE	SHOES	NOTES

RUNNING / JOGGING LOG

YEAR _______ MONTH _______

DATE	DISTANCE	TIME	PACE	HR	REST HR	RUN TYPE	SHOES	NOTES

SUNDAY
MONDAY
TUESDAY
WEDNESDAY
THURSDAY
FRIDAY
SATURDAY
NOTES
NOTES

RUNNING / JOGGING LOG

YEAR _______ MONTH _______

DATE	DISTANCE	TIME	PACE	HR	REST HR	RUN TYPE	SHOES	NOTES
DATE	DISTANCE	TIME	PACE	HR	REST HR	RUN TYPE	SHOES	NOTES

RUNNING / JOGGING LOG

YEAR _________ MONTH _________

DATE	DISTANCE	TIME	PACE	HR	REST HR	RUN TYPE	SHOES	NOTES
DATE	DISTANCE	TIME	PACE	HR	REST HR	RUN TYPE	SHOES	NOTES

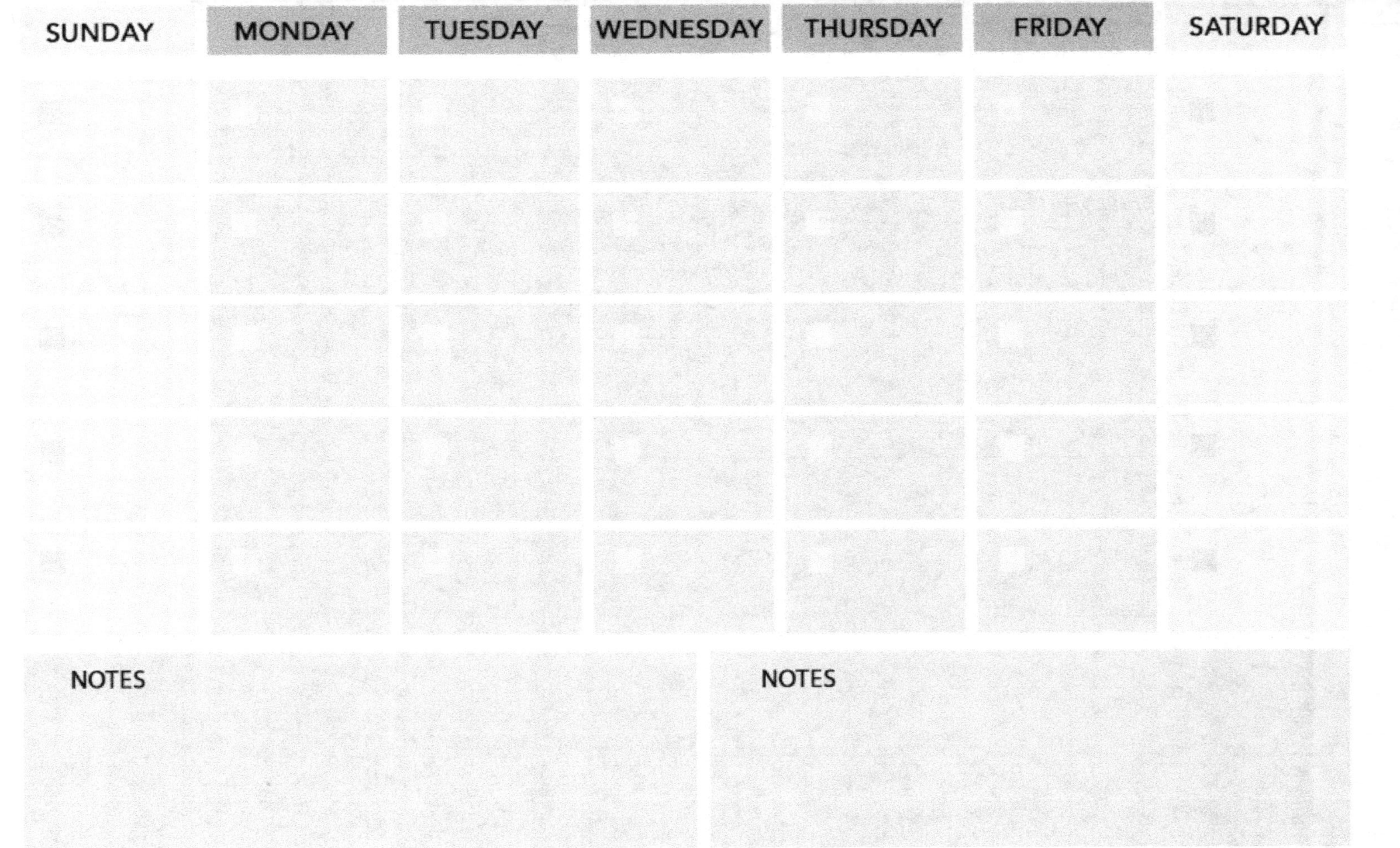

SUNDAY
MONDAY
TUESDAY
WEDNESDAY
THURSDAY
FRIDAY
SATURDAY
NOTES
NOTES

RUNNING / JOGGING LOG

YEAR _______ MONTH _______

DATE	DISTANCE	TIME	PACE	HR	REST HR	RUN TYPE	SHOES	NOTES
DATE	DISTANCE	TIME	PACE	HR	REST HR	RUN TYPE	SHOES	NOTES

RUNNING / JOGGING LOG

YEAR _________ MONTH _________

DATE	DISTANCE	TIME	PACE	HR	REST HR	RUN TYPE	SHOES	NOTES
DATE	DISTANCE	TIME	PACE	HR	REST HR	RUN TYPE	SHOES	NOTES

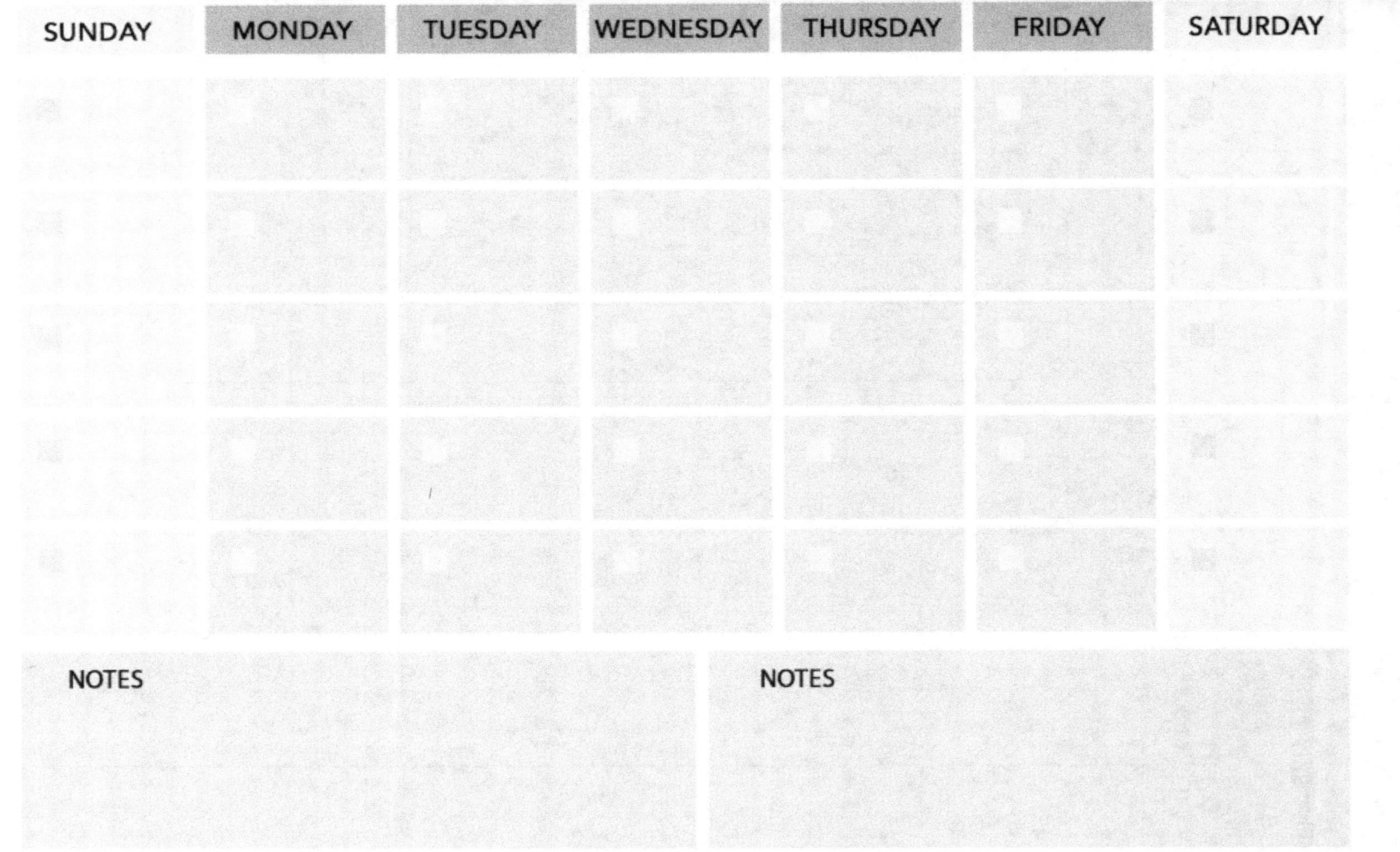

SUNDAY
MONDAY
TUESDAY
WEDNESDAY
THURSDAY
FRIDAY
SATURDAY
NOTES
NOTES

RUNNING / JOGGING LOG

YEAR _________ MONTH _________

DATE	DISTANCE	TIME	PACE	HR	REST HR	RUN TYPE	SHOES	NOTES

RUNNING / JOGGING LOG

YEAR _________ MONTH _________

DATE	DISTANCE	TIME	PACE	HR	REST HR	RUN TYPE	SHOES	NOTES
DATE	DISTANCE	TIME	PACE	HR	REST HR	RUN TYPE	SHOES	NOTES

SUNDAY	MONDAY	TUESDAY	WEDNESDAY	THURSDAY	FRIDAY	SATURDAY

NOTES

NOTES

RUNNING / JOGGING LOG

YEAR _________ MONTH _________

DATE	DISTANCE	TIME	PACE	HR	REST HR	RUN TYPE	SHOES	NOTES
DATE	DISTANCE	TIME	PACE	HR	REST HR	RUN TYPE	SHOES	NOTES

RUNNING / JOGGING LOG

YEAR _________ MONTH _________

DATE	DISTANCE	TIME	PACE	HR	REST HR	RUN TYPE	SHOES	NOTES
DATE	DISTANCE	TIME	PACE	HR	REST HR	RUN TYPE	SHOES	NOTES

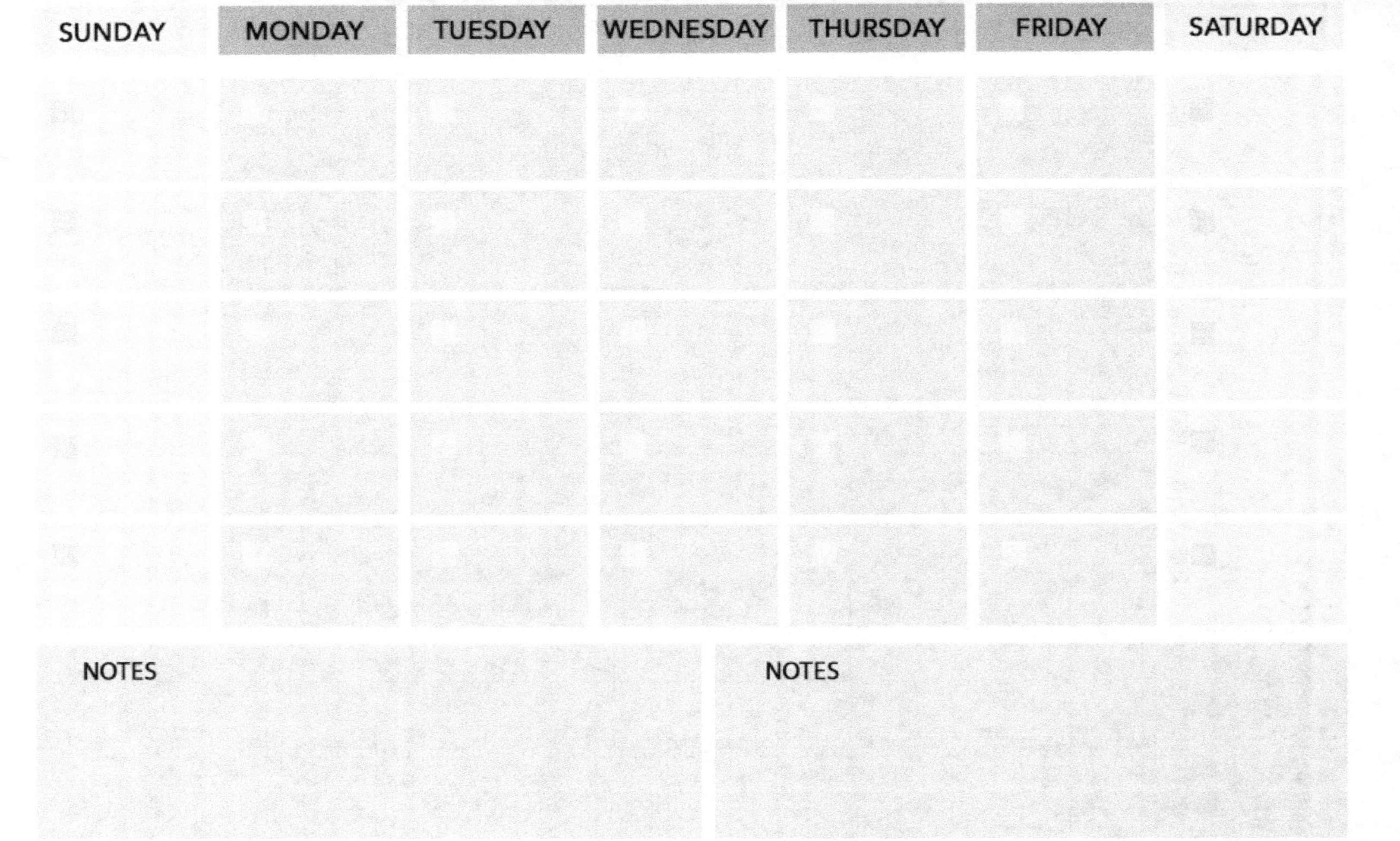
SUNDAY
MONDAY
TUESDAY
WEDNESDAY
THURSDAY
FRIDAY
SATURDAY
NOTES
NOTES

RUNNING / JOGGING LOG

YEAR _______ MONTH _______

DATE	DISTANCE	TIME	PACE	HR	REST HR	RUN TYPE	SHOES	NOTES
DATE	DISTANCE	TIME	PACE	HR	REST HR	RUN TYPE	SHOES	NOTES

RUNNING / JOGGING LOG

YEAR _______ MONTH _______

DATE	DISTANCE	TIME	PACE	HR	REST HR	RUN TYPE	SHOES	NOTES
DATE	DISTANCE	TIME	PACE	HR	REST HR	RUN TYPE	SHOES	NOTES

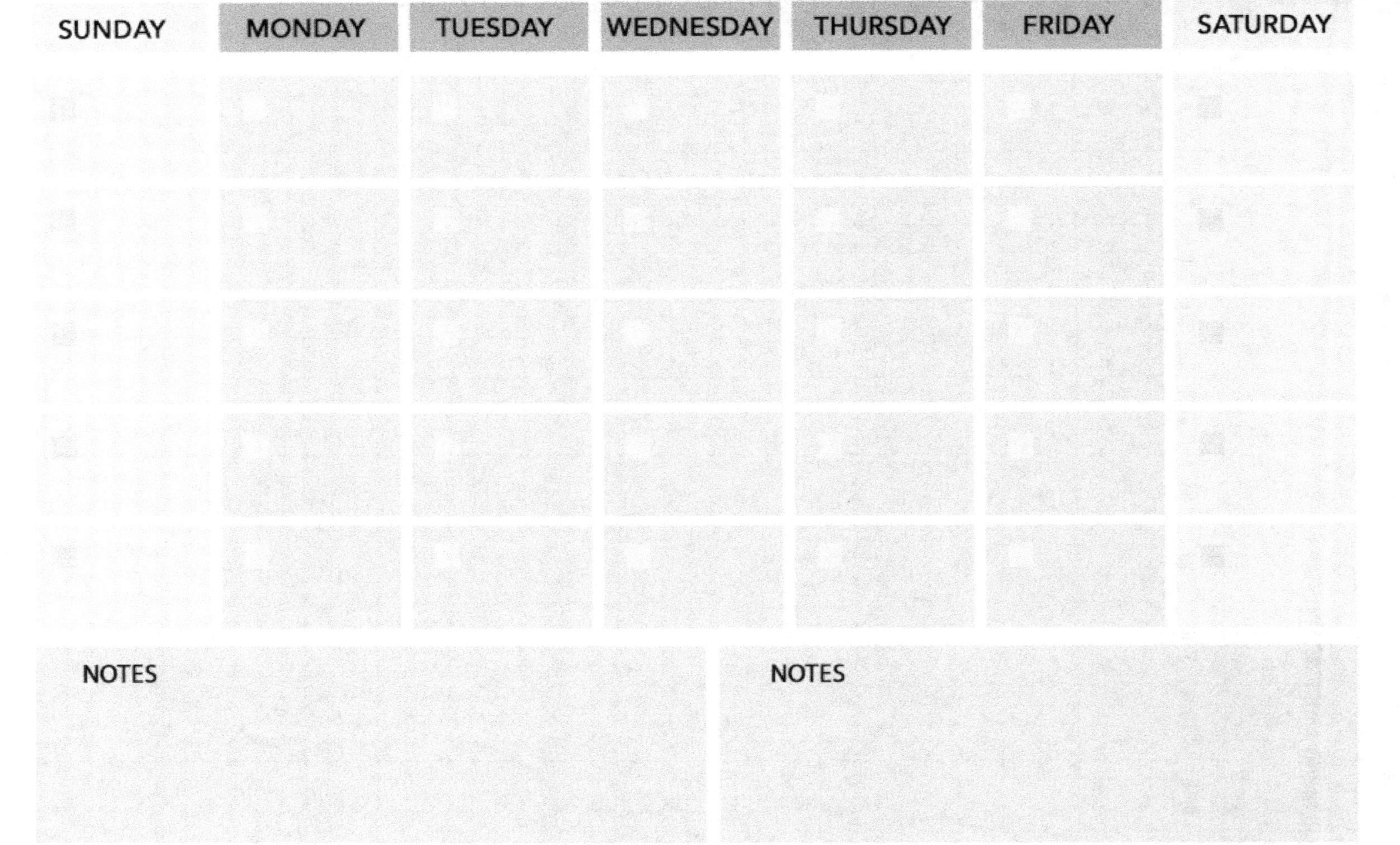

SUNDAY
MONDAY
TUESDAY
WEDNESDAY
THURSDAY
FRIDAY
SATURDAY
NOTES
NOTES

RUNNING / JOGGING LOG

YEAR _________ MONTH _________

DATE	DISTANCE	TIME	PACE	HR	REST HR	RUN TYPE	SHOES	NOTES

DATE	DISTANCE	TIME	PACE	HR	REST HR	RUN TYPE	SHOES	NOTES

RUNNING / JOGGING LOG

YEAR _________ MONTH _________

DATE	DISTANCE	TIME	PACE	HR	REST HR	RUN TYPE	SHOES	NOTES
DATE	DISTANCE	TIME	PACE	HR	REST HR	RUN TYPE	SHOES	NOTES

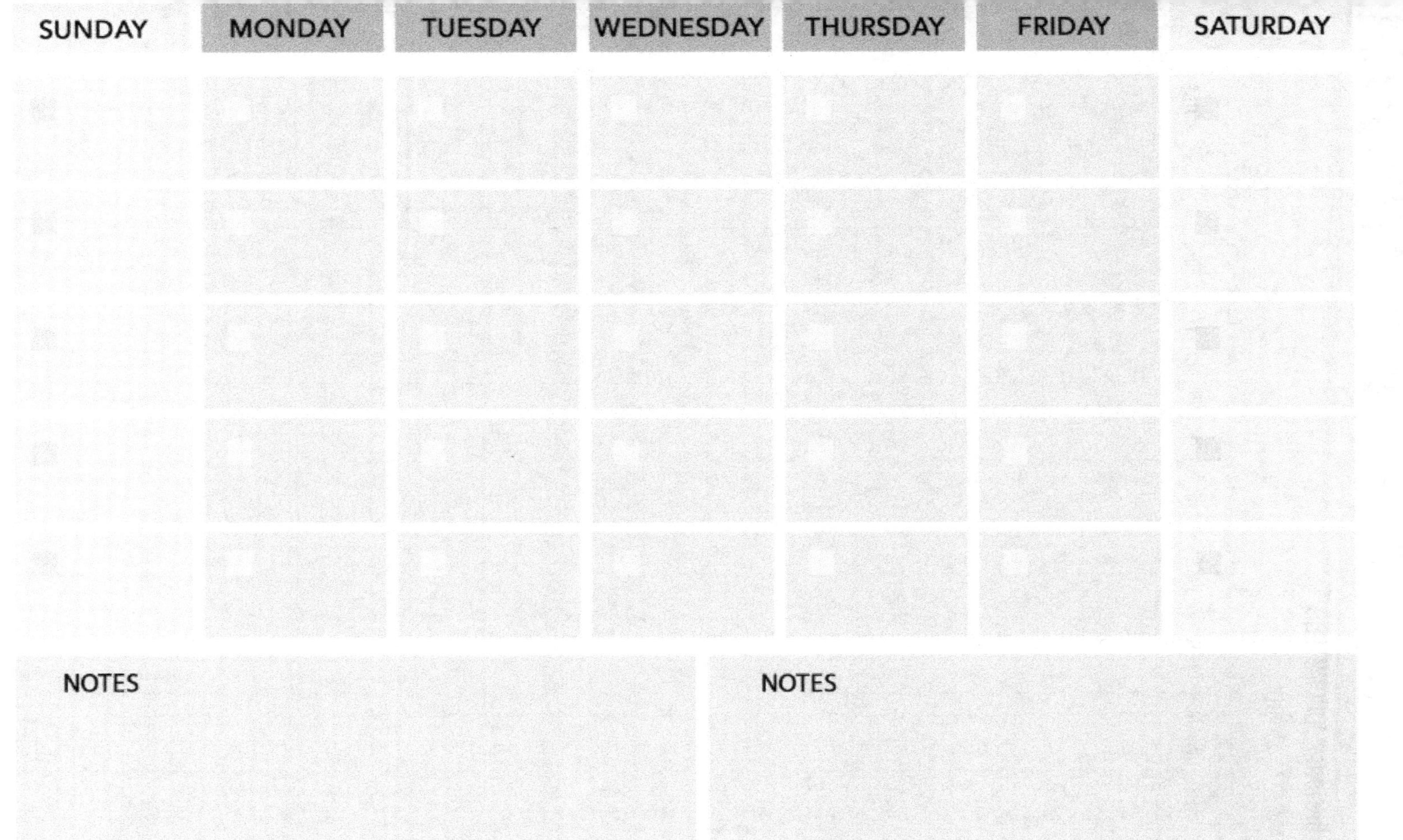
SUNDAY
MONDAY
TUESDAY
WEDNESDAY
THURSDAY
FRIDAY
SATURDAY
NOTES
NOTES

RUNNING / JOGGING LOG

YEAR _________ MONTH _________

DATE	DISTANCE	TIME	PACE	HR	REST HR	RUN TYPE	SHOES	NOTES
DATE	DISTANCE	TIME	PACE	HR	REST HR	RUN TYPE	SHOES	NOTES

RUNNING / JOGGING LOG

YEAR _______ MONTH _______

DATE	DISTANCE	TIME	PACE	HR	REST HR	RUN TYPE	SHOES	NOTES
DATE	DISTANCE	TIME	PACE	HR	REST HR	RUN TYPE	SHOES	NOTES

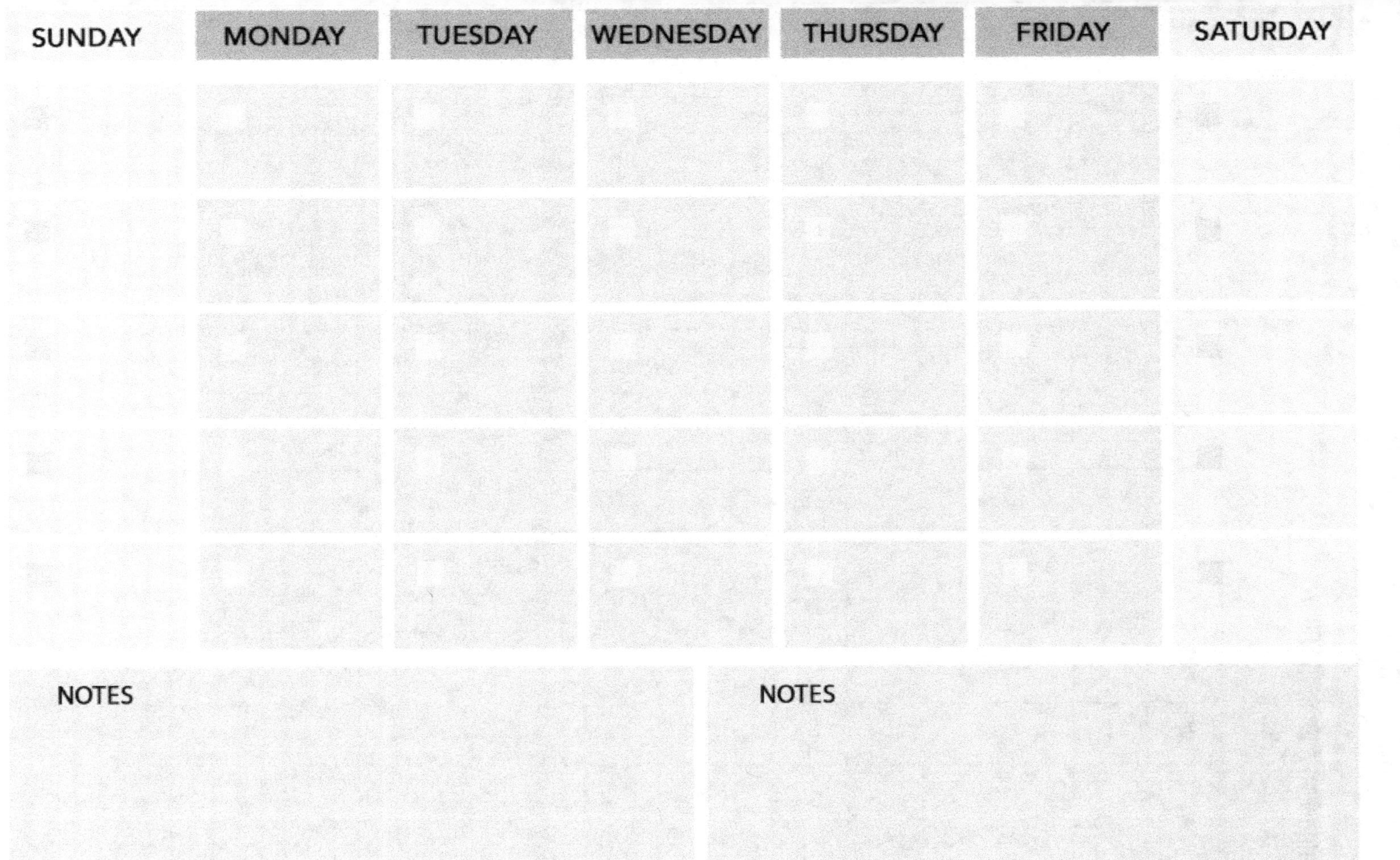

SUNDAY
MONDAY
TUESDAY
WEDNESDAY
THURSDAY
FRIDAY
SATURDAY
NOTES
NOTES

RUNNING / JOGGING LOG

YEAR _______ MONTH _______

DATE	DISTANCE	TIME	PACE	HR	REST HR	RUN TYPE	SHOES	NOTES
DATE	DISTANCE	TIME	PACE	HR	REST HR	RUN TYPE	SHOES	NOTES

RUNNING / JOGGING LOG

YEAR _______ MONTH _______

DATE	DISTANCE	TIME	PACE	HR	REST HR	RUN TYPE	SHOES	NOTES
DATE	DISTANCE	TIME	PACE	HR	REST HR	RUN TYPE	SHOES	NOTES

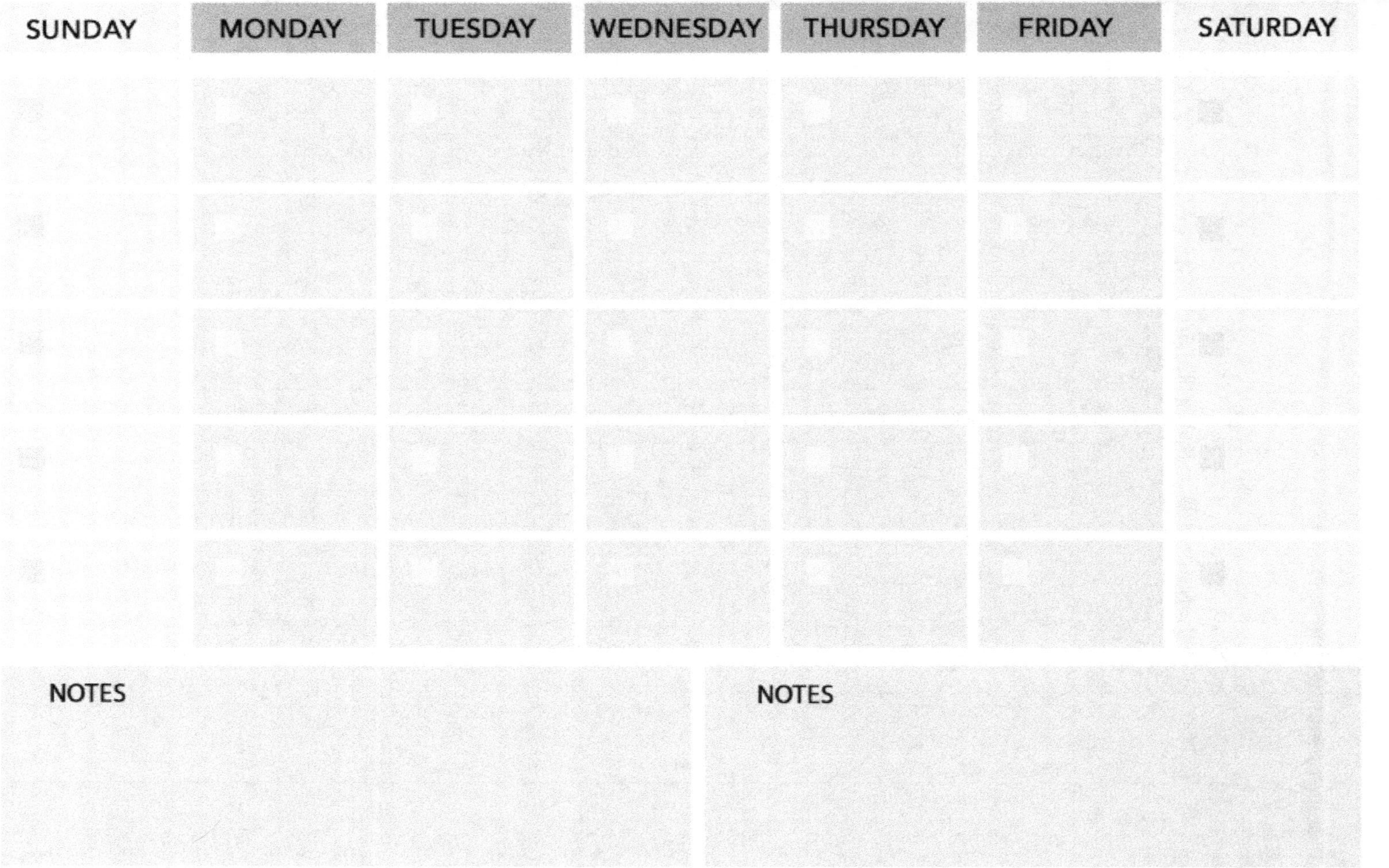

SUNDAY
MONDAY
TUESDAY
WEDNESDAY
THURSDAY
FRIDAY
SATURDAY
NOTES
NOTES

RUNNING / JOGGING LOG

YEAR _______ MONTH _______

DATE	DISTANCE	TIME	PACE	HR	REST HR	RUN TYPE	SHOES	NOTES
DATE	DISTANCE	TIME	PACE	HR	REST HR	RUN TYPE	SHOES	NOTES

RUNNING / JOGGING LOG

YEAR ________ MONTH ________

DATE	DISTANCE	TIME	PACE	HR	REST HR	RUN TYPE	SHOES	NOTES
DATE	DISTANCE	TIME	PACE	HR	REST HR	RUN TYPE	SHOES	NOTES

SUNDAY
MONDAY
TUESDAY
WEDNESDAY
THURSDAY
FRIDAY
SATURDAY
NOTES
NOTES

RUNNING / JOGGING LOG

YEAR _______ MONTH _______

DATE	DISTANCE	TIME	PACE	HR	REST HR	RUN TYPE	SHOES	NOTES
DATE	DISTANCE	TIME	PACE	HR	REST HR	RUN TYPE	SHOES	NOTES

RUNNING / JOGGING LOG

YEAR _______ MONTH _______

DATE	DISTANCE	TIME	PACE	HR	REST HR	RUN TYPE	SHOES	NOTES

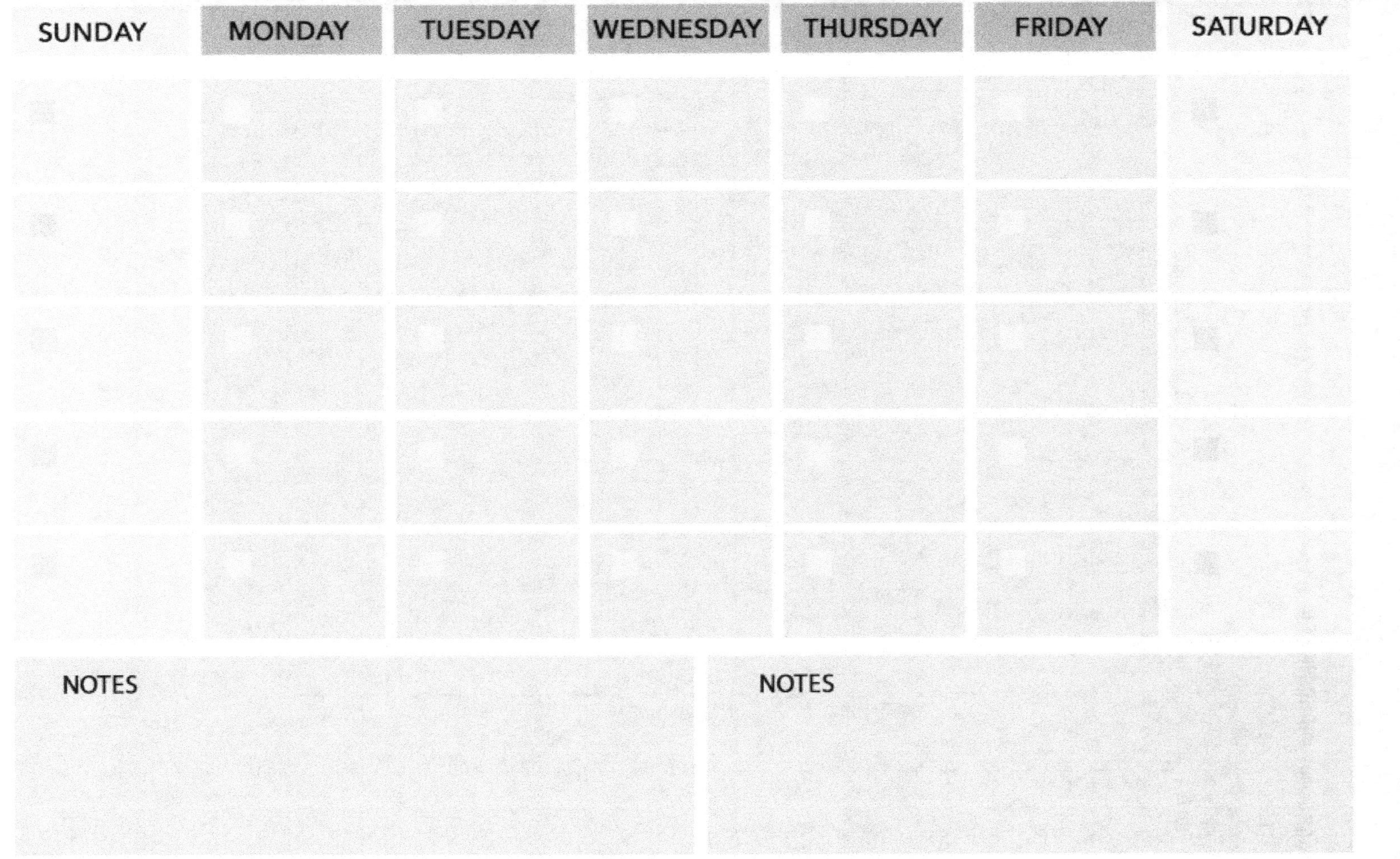

SUNDAY
MONDAY
TUESDAY
WEDNESDAY
THURSDAY
FRIDAY
SATURDAY
NOTES
NOTES

RUNNING / JOGGING LOG

YEAR _________ MONTH _________

DATE	DISTANCE	TIME	PACE	HR	REST HR	RUN TYPE	SHOES	NOTES

RUNNING / JOGGING LOG

YEAR _________ MONTH _________

DATE	DISTANCE	TIME	PACE	HR	REST HR	RUN TYPE	SHOES	NOTES
DATE	DISTANCE	TIME	PACE	HR	REST HR	RUN TYPE	SHOES	NOTES

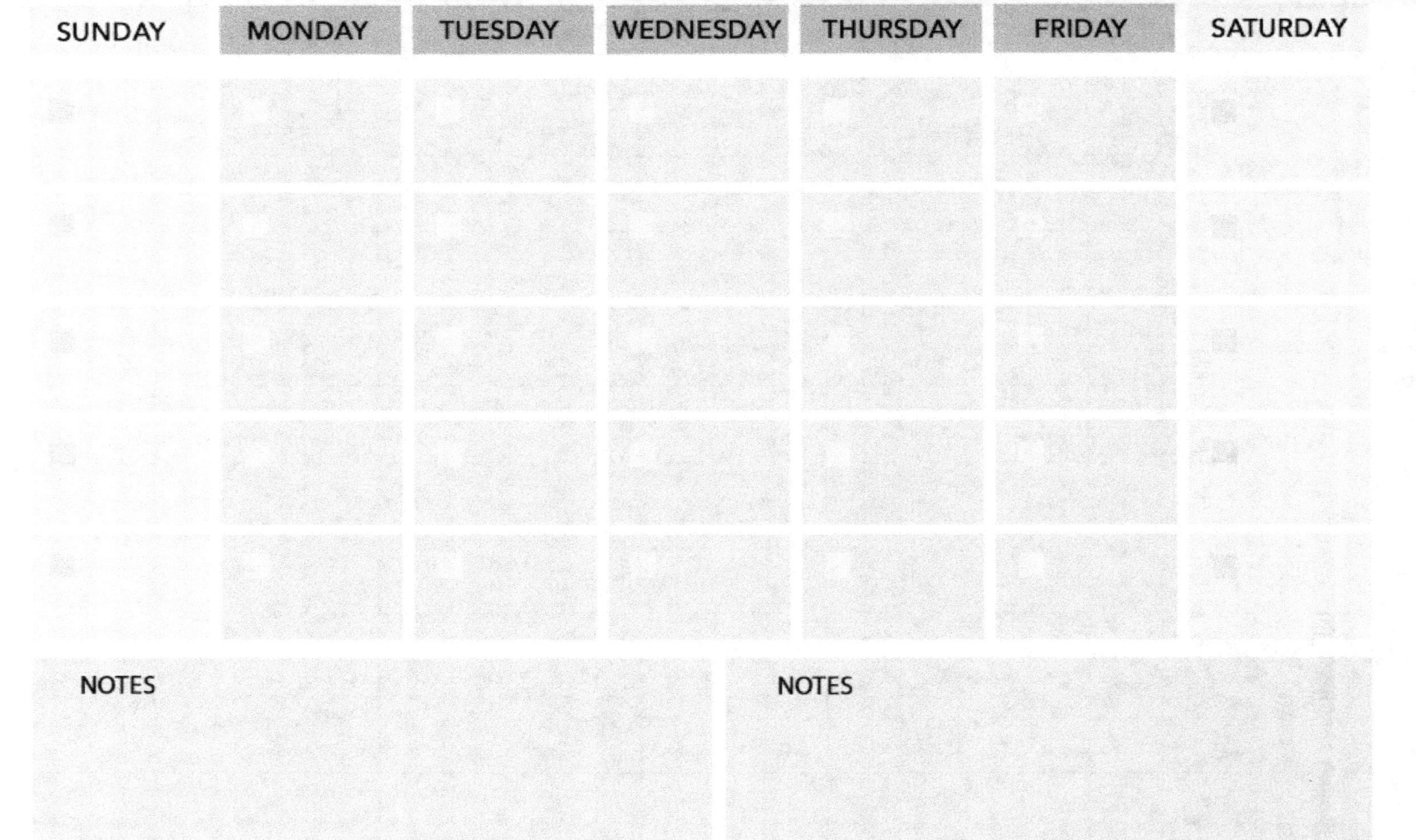

SUNDAY
MONDAY
TUESDAY
WEDNESDAY
THURSDAY
FRIDAY
SATURDAY
NOTES
NOTES

RUNNING / JOGGING LOG

YEAR ________ MONTH ________

DATE	DISTANCE	TIME	PACE	HR	REST HR	RUN TYPE	SHOES	NOTES
DATE	DISTANCE	TIME	PACE	HR	REST HR	RUN TYPE	SHOES	NOTES

RUNNING / JOGGING LOG

YEAR _______ MONTH _______

DATE	DISTANCE	TIME	PACE	HR	REST HR	RUN TYPE	SHOES	NOTES
DATE	DISTANCE	TIME	PACE	HR	REST HR	RUN TYPE	SHOES	NOTES

SUNDAY
MONDAY
TUESDAY
WEDNESDAY
THURSDAY
FRIDAY
SATURDAY
NOTES
NOTES

RUNNING / JOGGING LOG

YEAR _________ MONTH _________

DATE	DISTANCE	TIME	PACE	HR	REST HR	RUN TYPE	SHOES	NOTES

DATE	DISTANCE	TIME	PACE	HR	REST HR	RUN TYPE	SHOES	NOTES

RUNNING / JOGGING LOG

YEAR _________ MONTH _________

DATE	DISTANCE	TIME	PACE	HR	REST HR	RUN TYPE	SHOES	NOTES

SUNDAY	MONDAY	TUESDAY	WEDNESDAY	THURSDAY	FRIDAY	SATURDAY

NOTES

NOTES

RUNNING / JOGGING LOG

YEAR _________ MONTH _________

DATE	DISTANCE	TIME	PACE	HR	REST HR	RUN TYPE	SHOES	NOTES
DATE	DISTANCE	TIME	PACE	HR	REST HR	RUN TYPE	SHOES	NOTES

RUNNING / JOGGING LOG

YEAR _______ MONTH _______

DATE	DISTANCE	TIME	PACE	HR	REST HR	RUN TYPE	SHOES	NOTES
DATE	DISTANCE	TIME	PACE	HR	REST HR	RUN TYPE	SHOES	NOTES

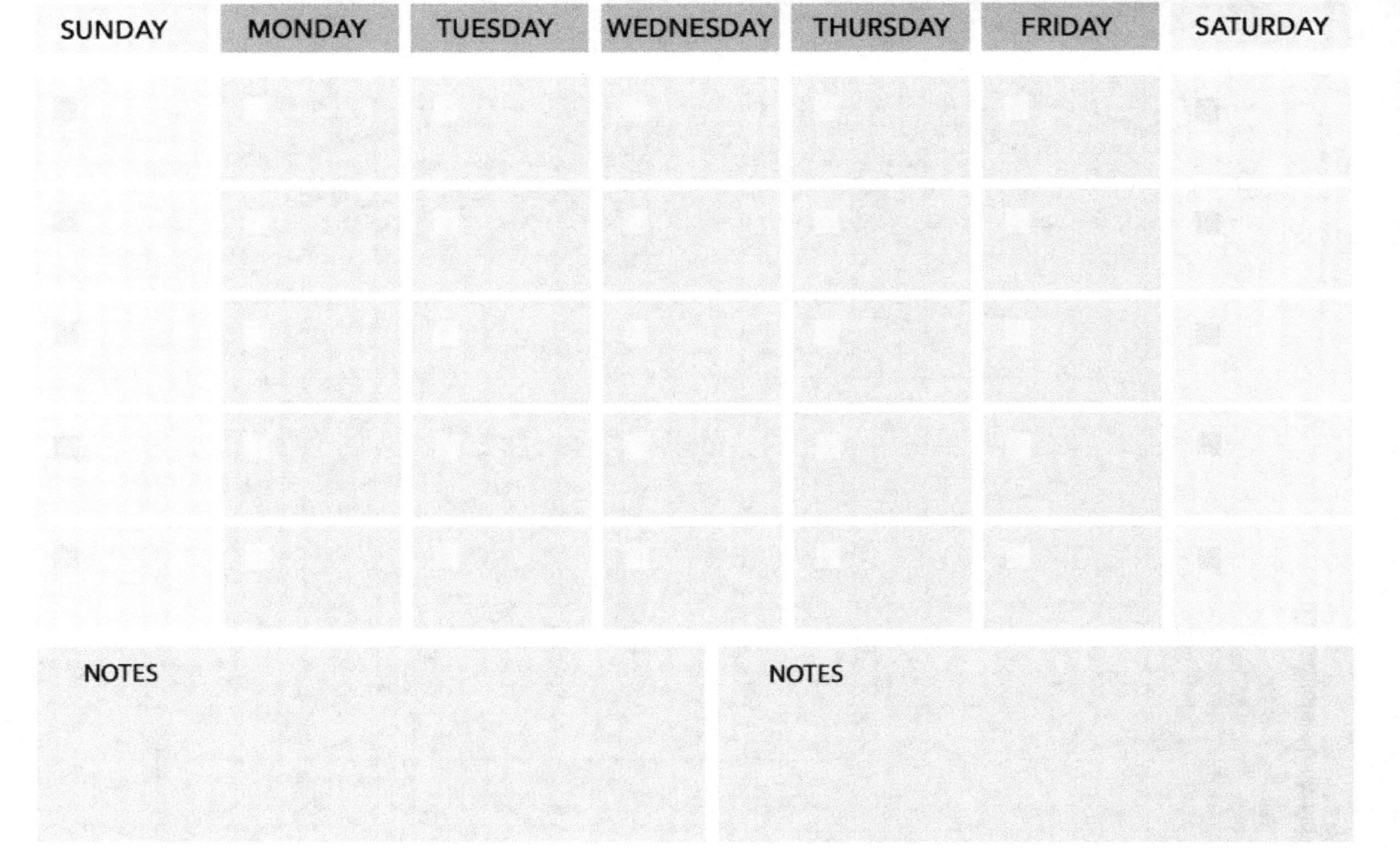

SUNDAY
MONDAY
TUESDAY
WEDNESDAY
THURSDAY
FRIDAY
SATURDAY
NOTES
NOTES

RUNNING / JOGGING LOG

YEAR _______ MONTH _______

DATE	DISTANCE	TIME	PACE	HR	REST HR	RUN TYPE	SHOES	NOTES
DATE	DISTANCE	TIME	PACE	HR	REST HR	RUN TYPE	SHOES	NOTES

RUNNING / JOGGING LOG

YEAR _________ MONTH _________

DATE	DISTANCE	TIME	PACE	HR	REST HR	RUN TYPE	SHOES	NOTES
DATE	DISTANCE	TIME	PACE	HR	REST HR	RUN TYPE	SHOES	NOTES

SUNDAY
MONDAY
TUESDAY
WEDNESDAY
THURSDAY
FRIDAY
SATURDAY
NOTES
NOTES

RUNNING / JOGGING LOG

YEAR _________ MONTH _________

DATE	DISTANCE	TIME	PACE	HR	REST HR	RUN TYPE	SHOES	NOTES
DATE	DISTANCE	TIME	PACE	HR	REST HR	RUN TYPE	SHOES	NOTES

RUNNING / JOGGING LOG

YEAR _______ MONTH _______

DATE	DISTANCE	TIME	PACE	HR	REST HR	RUN TYPE	SHOES	NOTES
DATE	DISTANCE	TIME	PACE	HR	REST HR	RUN TYPE	SHOES	NOTES

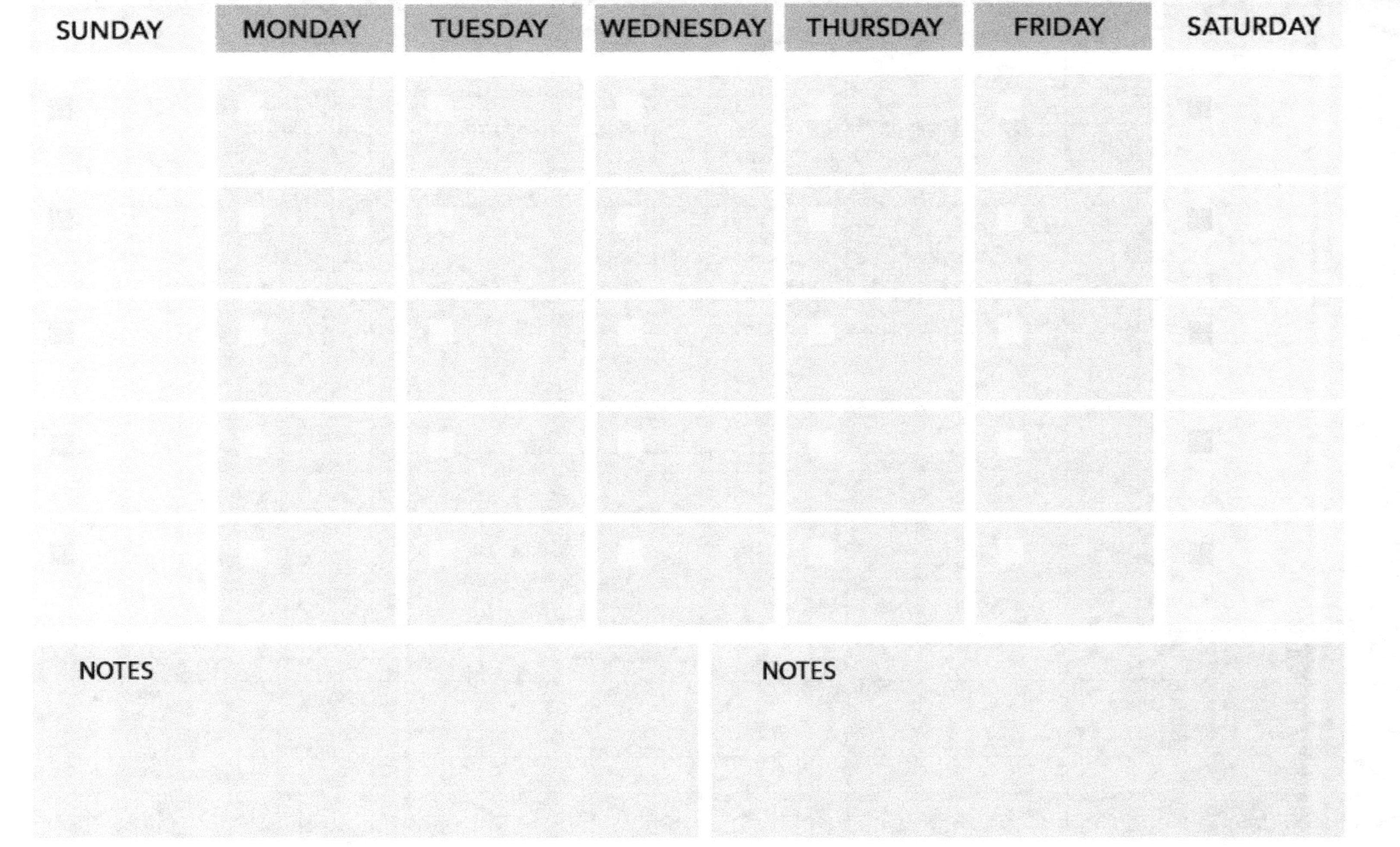

SUNDAY
MONDAY
TUESDAY
WEDNESDAY
THURSDAY
FRIDAY
SATURDAY
NOTES
NOTES

RUNNING / JOGGING LOG

YEAR _________ MONTH _________

DATE	DISTANCE	TIME	PACE	HR	REST HR	RUN TYPE	SHOES	NOTES

RUNNING / JOGGING LOG

YEAR _______ MONTH _______

DATE	DISTANCE	TIME	PACE	HR	REST HR	RUN TYPE	SHOES	NOTES

DATE	DISTANCE	TIME	PACE	HR	REST HR	RUN TYPE	SHOES	NOTES

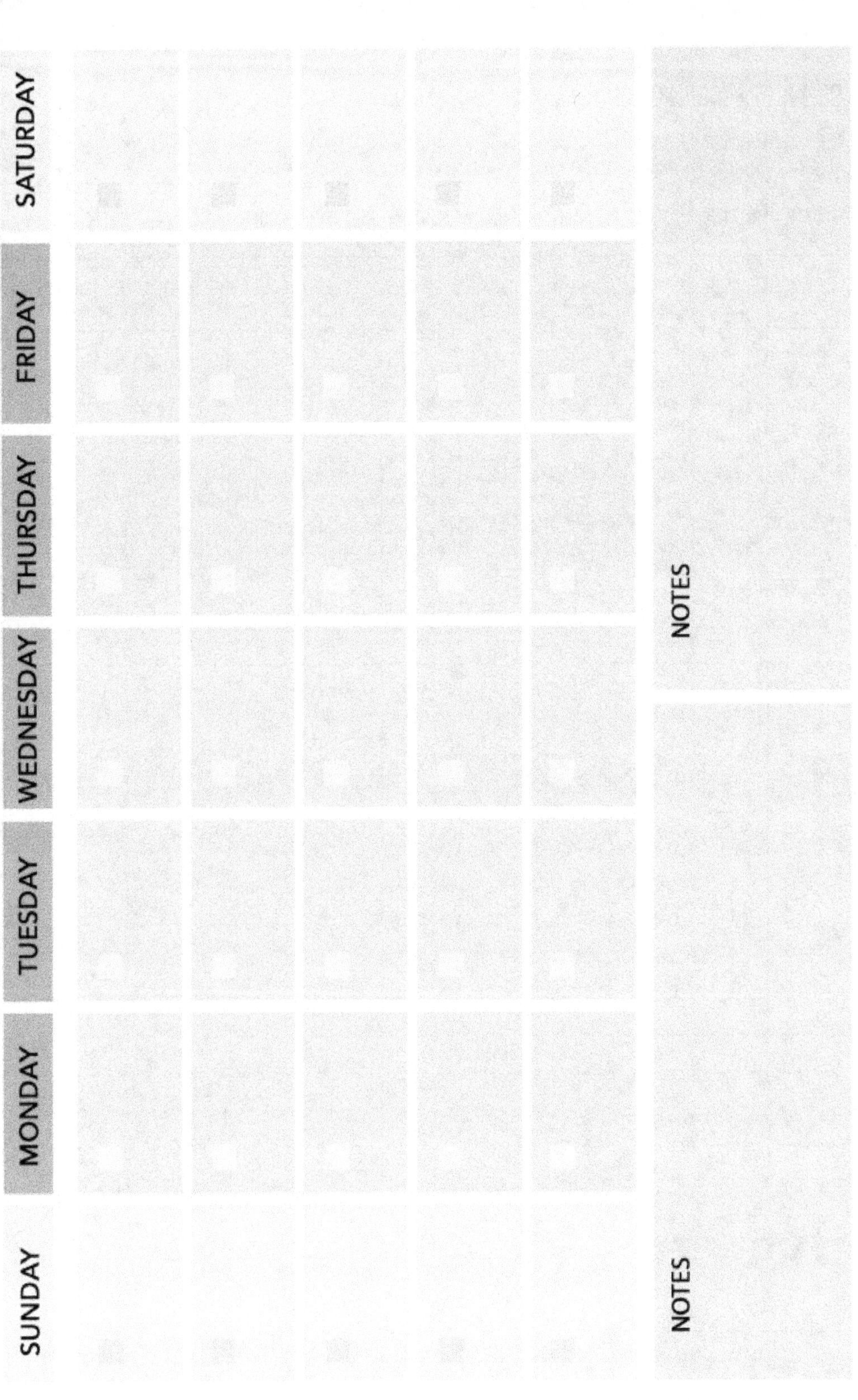

RUNNING / JOGGING LOG

YEAR _________ MONTH _________

DATE	DISTANCE	TIME	PACE	HR	REST HR	RUN TYPE	SHOES	NOTES

RUNNING / JOGGING LOG

YEAR _________ MONTH _________

DATE	DISTANCE	TIME	PACE	HR	REST HR	RUN TYPE	SHOES	NOTES

SUNDAY	MONDAY	TUESDAY	WEDNESDAY	THURSDAY	FRIDAY	SATURDAY

NOTES

NOTES

RUNNING / JOGGING LOG

YEAR _________ MONTH _________

DATE	DISTANCE	TIME	PACE	HR	REST HR	RUN TYPE	SHOES	NOTES
DATE	DISTANCE	TIME	PACE	HR	REST HR	RUN TYPE	SHOES	NOTES

RUNNING / JOGGING LOG

YEAR ________ MONTH ________

DATE	DISTANCE	TIME	PACE	HR	REST HR	RUN TYPE	SHOES	NOTES

DATE	DISTANCE	TIME	PACE	HR	REST HR	RUN TYPE	SHOES	NOTES

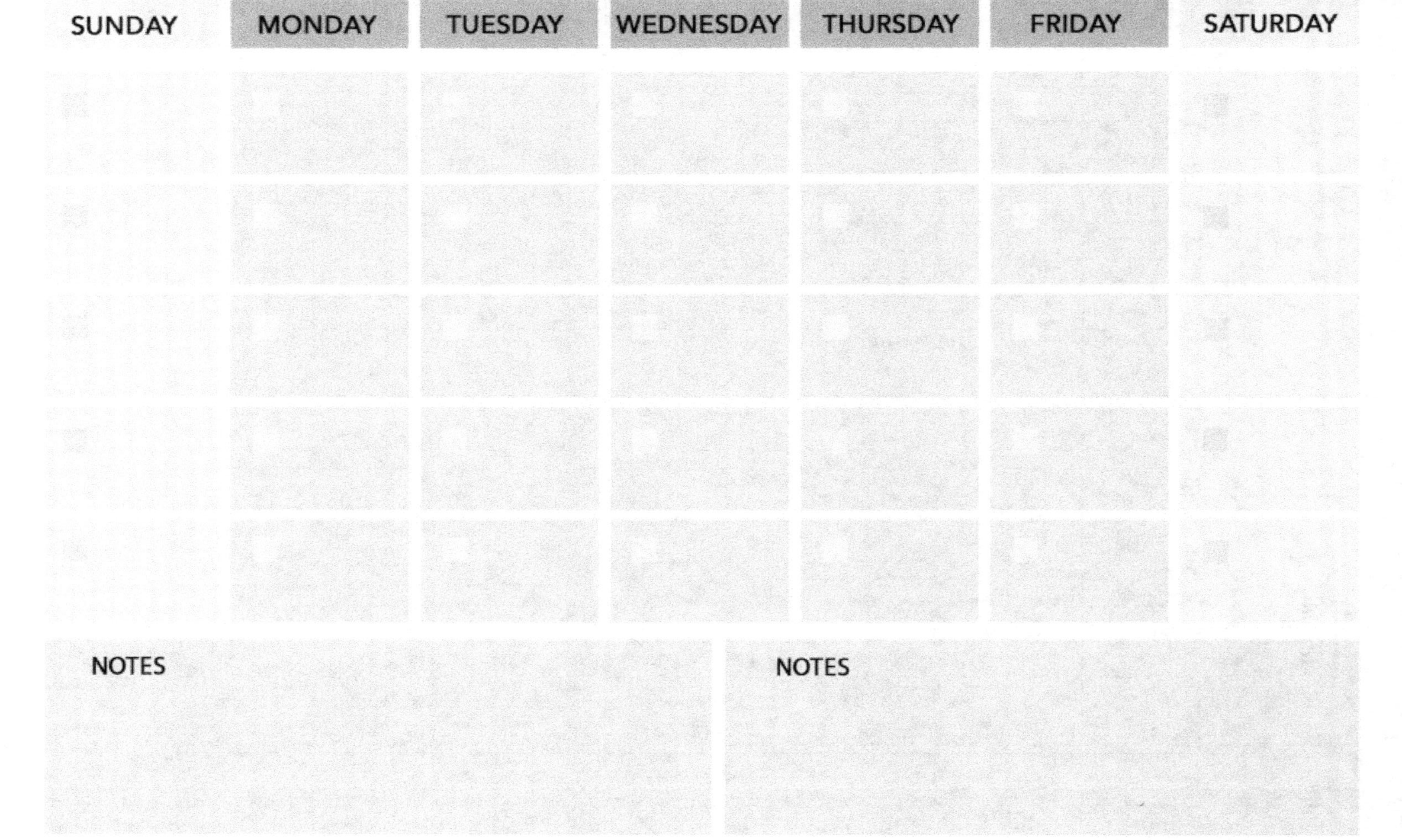

SUNDAY
MONDAY
TUESDAY
WEDNESDAY
THURSDAY
FRIDAY
SATURDAY
NOTES
NOTES

RUNNING / JOGGING LOG

YEAR _________ MONTH _________

DATE	DISTANCE	TIME	PACE	HR	REST HR	RUN TYPE	SHOES	NOTES
DATE	DISTANCE	TIME	PACE	HR	REST HR	RUN TYPE	SHOES	NOTES

RUNNING / JOGGING LOG

YEAR _________ MONTH _________

DATE	DISTANCE	TIME	PACE	HR	REST HR	RUN TYPE	SHOES	NOTES
DATE	DISTANCE	TIME	PACE	HR	REST HR	RUN TYPE	SHOES	NOTES

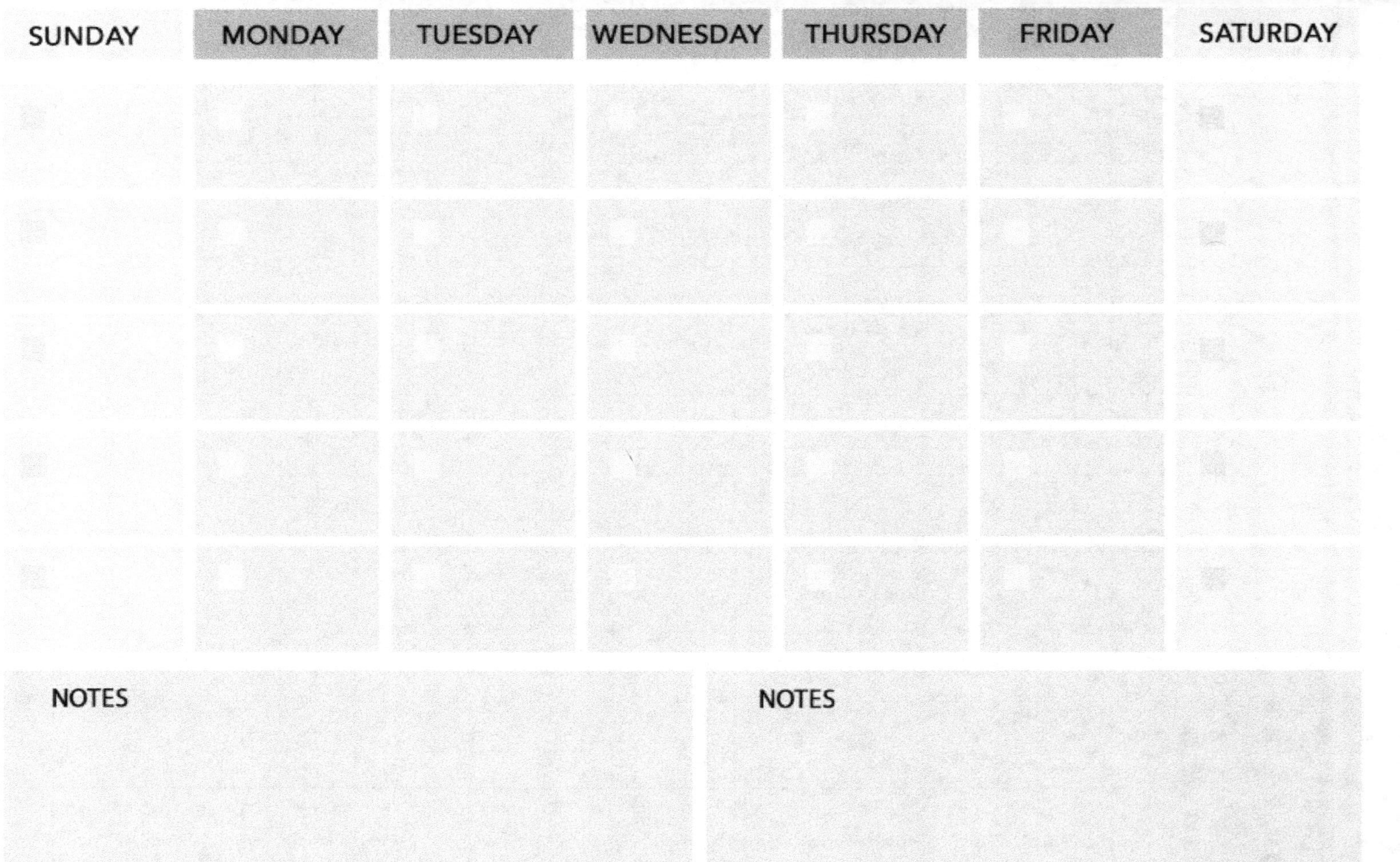

SUNDAY
MONDAY
TUESDAY
WEDNESDAY
THURSDAY
FRIDAY
SATURDAY
NOTES
NOTES

RUNNING / JOGGING LOG

YEAR _________ MONTH _________

DATE	DISTANCE	TIME	PACE	HR	REST HR	RUN TYPE	SHOES	NOTES
DATE	DISTANCE	TIME	PACE	HR	REST HR	RUN TYPE	SHOES	NOTES

RUNNING / JOGGING LOG

YEAR _________ MONTH _________

DATE	DISTANCE	TIME	PACE	HR	REST HR	RUN TYPE	SHOES	NOTES

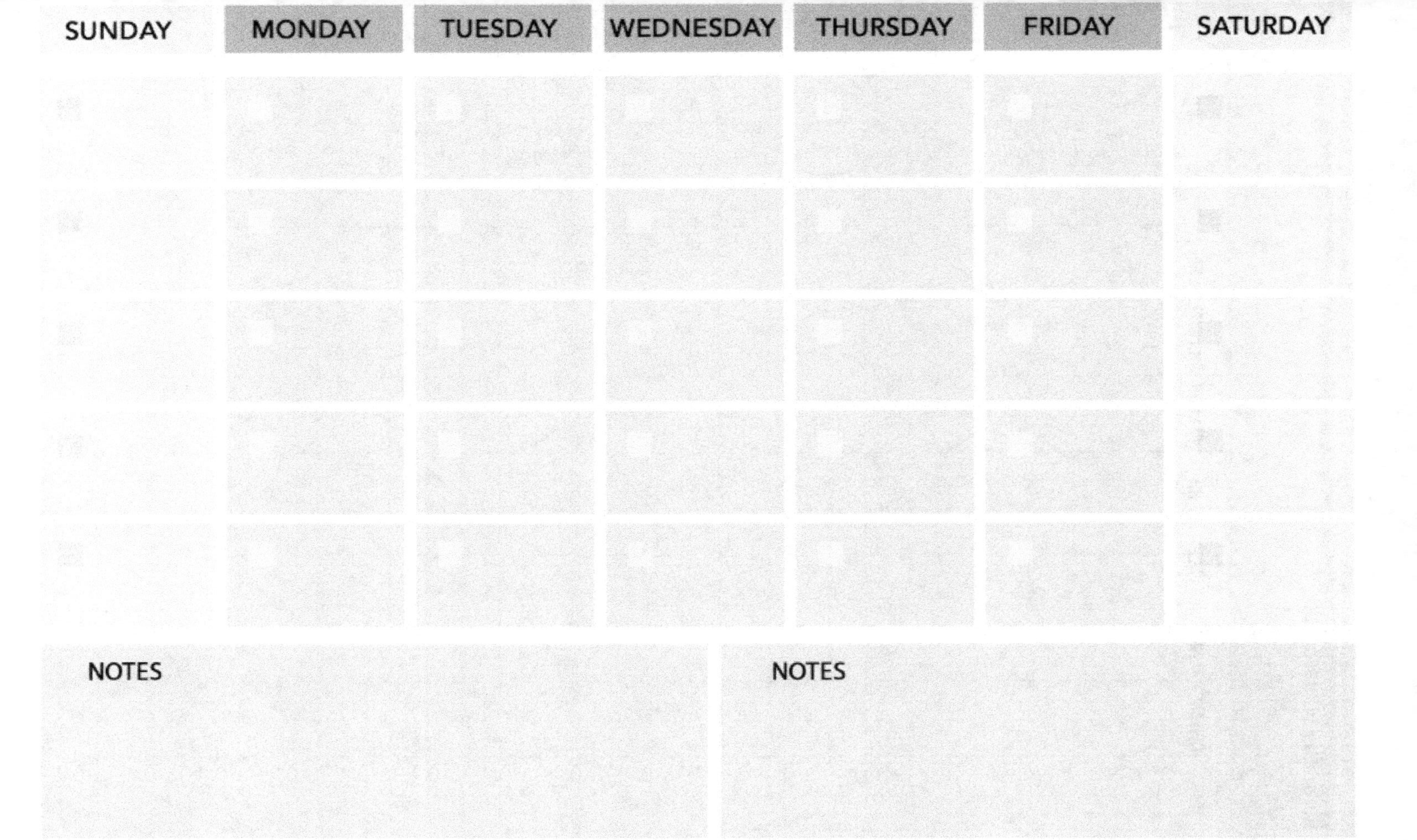
SUNDAY
MONDAY
TUESDAY
WEDNESDAY
THURSDAY
FRIDAY
SATURDAY
NOTES
NOTES

RUNNING / JOGGING LOG

YEAR _________ MONTH _________

DATE	DISTANCE	TIME	PACE	HR	REST HR	RUN TYPE	SHOES	NOTES

RUNNING / JOGGING LOG

YEAR _________ MONTH _________

DATE	DISTANCE	TIME	PACE	HR	REST HR	RUN TYPE	SHOES	NOTES

DATE	DISTANCE	TIME	PACE	HR	REST HR	RUN TYPE	SHOES	NOTES

SUNDAY
MONDAY
TUESDAY
WEDNESDAY
THURSDAY
FRIDAY
SATURDAY
NOTES
NOTES

RUNNING / JOGGING LOG

YEAR _________ MONTH _________

DATE	DISTANCE	TIME	PACE	HR	REST HR	RUN TYPE	SHOES	NOTES
DATE	DISTANCE	TIME	PACE	HR	REST HR	RUN TYPE	SHOES	NOTES

RUNNING / JOGGING LOG

YEAR _______ MONTH _______

DATE	DISTANCE	TIME	PACE	HR	REST HR	RUN TYPE	SHOES	NOTES
DATE	DISTANCE	TIME	PACE	HR	REST HR	RUN TYPE	SHOES	NOTES

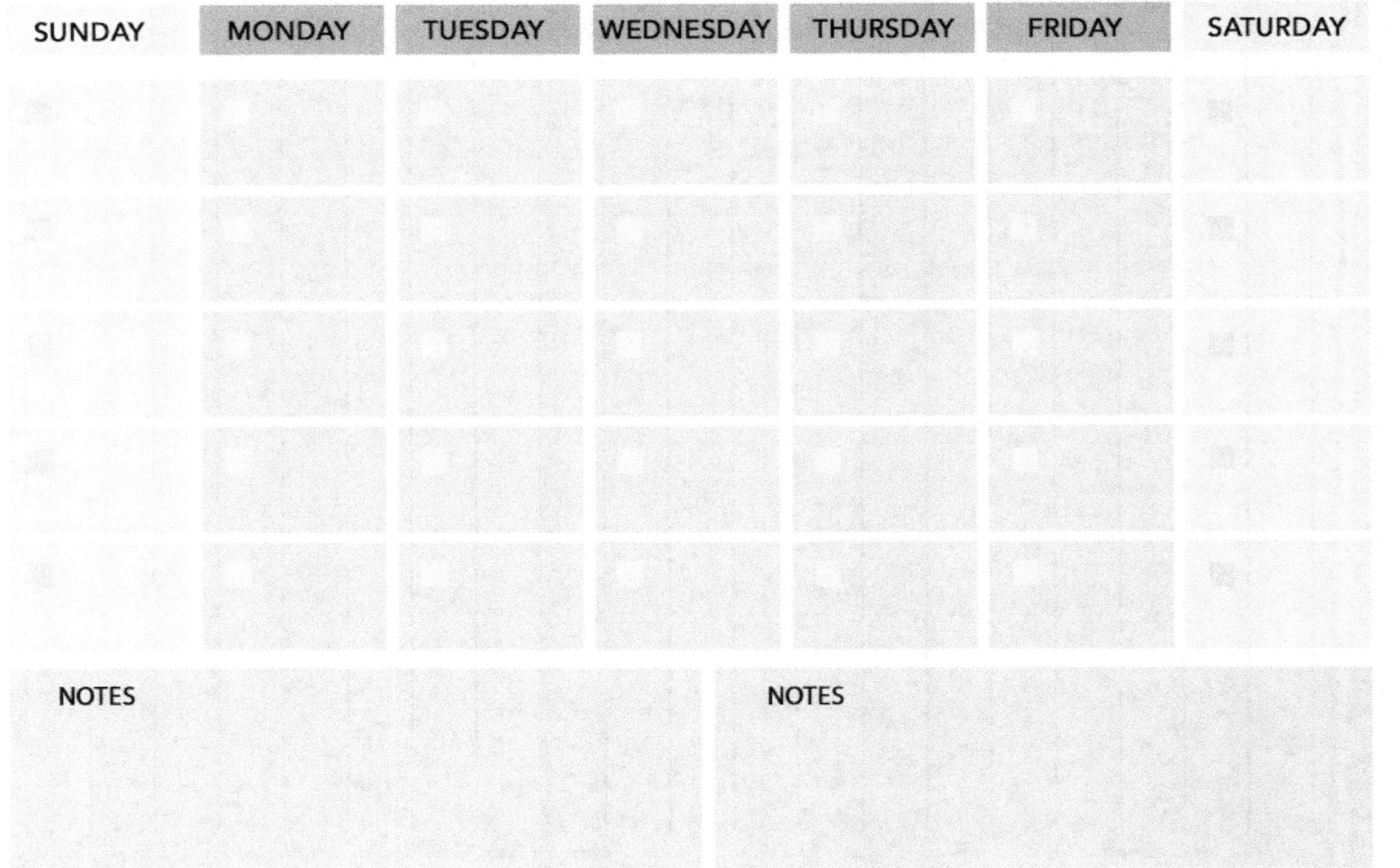

SUNDAY
MONDAY
TUESDAY
WEDNESDAY
THURSDAY
FRIDAY
SATURDAY
NOTES
NOTES